D1378297

Careers in Focus

ART

SECOND EDITION

Ferguson

An imprint of Infobase Publishing

Careers in Focus: Art, Second Edition

Copyright © 2008 by Infobase Publishing

Ferguson
An imprint of Infobase Publishing
132 West 31st Street
New York NY 10001

Library of Congress Cataloging-in-Publication Data

Careers in focus. Art. — 2nd ed.
   p. cm.
  Includes bibliographical references and index.
  ISBN-13: 978-0-8160-7283-5 (alk. paper)
  ISBN-10: 0-8160-7283-3 (alk. paper)
  1. Art—Vocational guidance—Juvenile literature. I. Ferguson Publishing. II. Title: Art.
  N8350.C37 2008
  702.3'73—dc22
                   2008001749

Ferguson books are available at special discounts when purchased in bulk quantities for businesses, associations, institutions, or sales promotions. Please call our Special Sales Department in New York at (212) 967-8800 or (800) 322-8755.

You can find Ferguson on the World Wide Web at http://www.fergpubco.com

Text design by David Strelecky
Cover design by Salvatore Luongo

Printed in the United States of America

Sheridan MSRF 10 9 8 7 6 5 4 3 2 1

This book is printed on acid-free paper.

Table of Contents

Introduction

Although some might associate an art career with years spent trying to avoid the "starving artist" lifestyle, this is hardly the case. An artistic inclination can serve as a gateway to any number of rewarding and exciting careers. Gone are the days when being an artist meant toiling in front of canvases or sculpture in an effort to escape creative obscurity and put bread on the table. Today, many individuals have found ways to turn their creative abilities into successful careers while still making time for personal creative efforts in their off time. Today's artists work in large corporations, schools, theaters, hospitals, museums, and their own homes. Although some artists make their living strictly through their creative works, most individuals in this field combine their creativity with some sort of technical skill, such as computer design, or specialized training, such as counseling, in order to pursue their career goals.

The field of art is roughly divided into three categories: commercial art, fine art, and craft. Commercial art, such as graphic design and illustration, is used in advertising agencies, publishing companies, and other businesses to attract attention and convey messages. Fine art, such as painting, sculpting, and calligraphy, is created more for personal expression than financial gain, although it can be financially rewarding. Craft refers to the generation of art objects that serve a function, such as jewelry making and sewing. Other careers for artists, such as conservation, art therapy, and teaching art, would fall under the veil of other fields, but these still require a true artistic sensibility.

Each article in *Careers in Focus: Art* discusses a particular art occupation in detail. The articles appear in Ferguson's *Encyclopedia of Careers and Vocational Guidance,* but have been updated and revised with the latest information from the U.S. Department of Labor, professional organizations, and other sources. In addition, the following new articles have been written specifically for this book: Gallery Owners and Directors and Visual Artists.

The following paragraphs detail the sections and features that appear in the book.

The **Quick Facts** section provides a brief summary of the career, including recommended school subjects, personal skills, work environment, minimum educational requirements, salary ranges, certification or licensing requirements, and employment outlook. This section also provides acronyms and identification numbers for the following government classification indexes: the *Dictionary of Occupational Titles* (DOT), the *Guide for Occupational Exploration* (GOE), the National Occupational Classification (NOC) Index, and the Occupational Information Network (O*NET)-Standard Occupational Classification System (SOC) index. The DOT, GOE, and O*NET-SOC indexes have been created by the U.S. government; the NOC index is Canada's career classification system. Readers can use the identification numbers listed in the Quick Facts section to access further information about a career. Print editions of the DOT (*Dictionary of Occupational Titles*. Indianapolis, Ind.: JIST Works, 1991) and GOE (*Guide for Occupational Exploration*. Indianapolis, Ind.: JIST Works, 2001) are available at libraries. Electronic versions of the NOC (http://www23.hrdc-drhc.gc.ca) and O*NET-SOC (http://online.onetcenter.org) are available on the Internet. When no DOT, GOE, NOC, or O*NET-SOC numbers are present, this means that the U.S. Department of Labor or Human Resources Development Canada have not created a numerical designation for this career. In this instance, you will see the acronym "N/A," or not available.

The **Overview** section is a brief introductory description of the duties and responsibilities involved in this career. Oftentimes, a career may have a variety of job titles. When this is the case, alternative career titles are presented. Employment statistics are also provided, when available. The **History** section describes the history of the particular job as it relates to the overall development of its industry or field. **The Job** describes the primary and secondary duties of the job. **Requirements** discusses high school and postsecondary education and training requirements, any certification or licensing that is necessary, and other personal requirements for success in the job. **Exploring** offers suggestions on how to gain experience in or knowledge of the particular job before making a firm educational and financial commitment. The focus is on what can be done while still in high school (or in the early years of college) to gain a better understanding of the job. The **Employers** section gives an overview of typical places of employment for the job. **Starting Out** discusses the best ways to land that first job, be it through the college career services office, newspaper ads, Internet employment sites, or personal contact. The **Advancement** section describes what kind of career path to expect from the job and how to get there. **Earnings** lists salary ranges and describes the typical fringe benefits. The **Work Environment** section describes the typical surroundings and conditions of employment—whether indoors or outdoors, noisy or quiet, social or independent. Also discussed are typical hours worked, any seasonal fluctuations, and the stresses and strains of the job. The **Outlook** section summarizes the job in terms of the general economy and industry projections. For the most part, Outlook information is obtained from the U.S. Bureau of Labor Statistics and is supplemented by information gathered from professional associations. Job growth terms follow those used in the *Occupational Outlook Handbook*. Growth described as "much faster than the average" means an increase of 27 percent or more. Growth described as "faster than the average" means an increase of 18 to 26 percent. Growth described as "about as fast as the average" means an increase of 9 to 17 percent. Growth described as "more slowly than the average" means an increase of 0 to 8 percent. "Decline" means a decrease by any amount. Each article ends with **For More Information,** which lists organizations that provide information on training, education, internships, scholarships, and job placement.

Careers in Focus: Art also includes photographs, informative sidebars, and interviews with professionals in the field.

Antiques and Art Dealers

OVERVIEW

Antiques and art dealers make a living acquiring, displaying, and selling antiques and art. By strict definition, antiques are often defined as items more than 100 years old. However, over the last two decades, the term "antique" has been applied to furniture, jewelry, clothing, art, household goods, and many other collectibles, dating back to as recently as the 1970s. People collect a wide array of items, from traditional paintings and sculptures to unique period toys and cigar boxes. Many antiques and art dealers are self-employed and go into business after discovering an interest in collecting pieces themselves. The Antiques and Collectibles National Association estimates there are approximately 200,000 to 250,000 antique dealers in the United States, based in antique shops, antique malls, and on the Internet.

HISTORY

Interest in collecting antiques and art can be traced back to the Renaissance, when people began to admire and prize Greek and Roman antiquities such as coins, manuscripts, sculptures, paintings, and pieces of architecture. In order to fulfill public interest and curiosity, as well as to supply the growing number of private and public collections, many pieces from Egypt, Italy, and Greece were looted and carried off to other countries.

The collectibles market, as it is known today, consists of everyday household objects, as well as furniture, clothing, art, and even

QUICK FACTS

School Subjects
Art
Art History
Business

Personal Skills
Artistic
Leadership/management

Work Environment
Primarily indoors
Primarily multiple locations

Minimum Education Level
High school diploma

Salary Range
$15,000 to $30,000 to $1 million

Certification or Licensing
None available

Outlook
About as fast as the average

DOT
N/A

GOE
N/A

NOC
0621

O*NET-SOC
N/A

automobiles, usually originating from another time period. After World War I, interest in collectibles grew. Many people began to purchase, preserve, and display pieces in their homes. As interest grew, so did the need for antiques and art businesses and dealers.

There are different categories of collectibles and different ways and reasons to acquire them. Some people choose to collect pieces from different time periods such as American Colonial or Victorian; others collect by the pattern or brand, such as Chippendale furniture or Coca-Cola memorabilia. Some people collect objects related to their career or business. For example, a physician may collect early surgical instruments, while a pharmacist may be interested in antique apothecary cabinets. A growing category in the collectibles industry is ephemera. Ephemera include theater programs, postcards, cigarette cards, and food labels, among others. These items were produced without lasting value or survival in mind. Though many pieces of ephemera can be purchased inexpensively, others, especially items among the first of their kind or in excellent condition, are rare and considered very valuable.

Some larger antiques and art dealers specialize and deal only with items from a particular time period or design. However, most dealers collect, buy, and sell all kinds of previously owned household items and decor. Such shops will carry items ranging from dining room furniture to jewelry to cooking molds.

The idea of what is worth collecting constantly changes with time and the public's tastes and interests. Art tastes range from traditional to contemporary, from Picasso to Warhol. Items representing the rock music industry of the 1960s and 1970s, as well as household items and furniture of the 1970s, are highly sought after today. Dealers not only stock their stores with items currently in demand but keep an eye on the collectibles of the future.

THE JOB

For Sandra Naujokas, proprietor of Favorite Things Antique Shop, in Orland Park, Illinois, the antiques business is never boring. More than 25 years ago, she started a collection of English-style china, and she's been hooked on antiques and collecting ever since. Naujokas spends her workday greeting customers and answering any questions they may have. When business slows down, she cleans the store and prices inventory. Sometimes people will bring in items for resale. It's up to Naujokas to carefully inspect each piece and settle on a price. She relies on pricing manuals such as *Kovels' Antiques & Collectibles Price List* and *Schroeder's Antiques Price Guide,* which give guidelines and a suggested price on a wide range of items.

Art dealers review documentation for various works of art before an art show. *(Jeff Greenberg, The Image Works)*

Naujokas also goes on a number of shopping expeditions each year to restock her store. Besides rummage sales and auctions, she relies on buying trips to different parts of the country and abroad to find regional items. At times, she is invited to a person's home to view items for sale. "It's important to be open to all possibilities," Naujokas says.

She also participates in several shows a year in order to reach customers who normally would not travel to the store's location. "You need to do a variety of things to advertise your wares," Naujokas advises.

She also promotes her business by advertising in her town's travel brochure, the local newspapers, and by direct mail campaigns. Her schedule is grueling, as the store is open seven days a week, but Naujokas enjoys the work and the challenge of being an antiques dealer. Besides the social aspect—interacting with all sorts of people and situations—Naujokas loves having the first choice of items for her personal collections. Her advice for people interested in having their own antique store? "You have to really like the items you intend to sell."

REQUIREMENTS

High School

You can become an antiques or art dealer with a high school diploma, though many successful dealers have become specialists in their field partly through further education. While in high school, concentrate on history and art classes to familiarize yourself with the particular significance and details of different periods in time and the corresponding art of the period. Consider studying home economics if you plan to specialize in household items. This knowledge can come in handy when distinguishing a wooden rolling pin from a wooden butter paddle, for example.

English and speech classes to improve communication skills are also helpful. Antiques and art dealing is a people-oriented business. For this reason, it's crucial to be able to deal efficiently with different types of people and situations. Operating your own small business will also require skills such as accounting, simple bookkeeping, and marketing, so business classes are recommended.

Postsecondary Training

While a college education is not required, a degree in fine arts, art history, or history will give you a working knowledge of the antiques you sell and the historical periods from which they originate. Another option is obtaining a degree in business or entrepreneurship. Such knowledge will help you to run a successful business.

Certification or Licensing

Presently, there are no certification programs available for antiques dealers. However, if you plan to open your own antique store, you will need a local business license or permit.

In addition, if you wish to conduct appraisals, it will be necessary to take appraisal courses that are appropriate for your interest or antique specialty. Certification is not required of those interested in working as an appraiser, but it is highly recommended, according to the International Society of Appraisers—which administers an accreditation and certification program to its members. Obtaining accreditation or certification will demonstrate your knowledge and expertise in appraisal and attract customers. To obtain accreditation, candidates must have three years of experience in appraising, complete the ISA Core Course in Appraisal Studies, and pass an examination. In order to become certified, individuals must complete additional training in their specialty area, submit two appraisals for peer review, complete professional development study, and pass a comprehensive examination.

Other Requirements

To be an antiques or art dealer, you'll need patience—and lots of it. Keeping your store well stocked with antiques, art, or other collectibles takes numerous buying trips to auctions, estate sales, flea markets, rummage sales, and even to foreign countries. Many times you'll have to sort through boxes of ordinary "stuff" before coming across a treasure. Unless you're lucky enough to have a large staff, you will have to make these outings by yourself. However, most dealers go into the profession because they enjoy the challenge of hunting for valuable pieces.

In addition to being patient in the hunt for treasure, art dealers also have to be patient when dealing with clients. Works of art can cost thousands, even millions of dollars; as a result, purchases are typically not quick decisions. The ability to work with a client over some time and gradually persuade them to invest in a piece takes time, skill, and patience.

Tact is another must-have quality for success in this industry. Remember the old adage—one person's trash is another person's treasure.

Finally, with the growth of online auction sites such as eBay, computer skills have come to be an essential part of the antique or collectible dealer's toolkit.

EXPLORING

To explore this field further, you may want to start by visiting an antique store or art gallery. If you see valuable treasures as opposed to dull paintings, old furniture, outdated books, or dusty collectibles, then chances are this is the job for you.

You can also tune to an episode of public television's traveling antique show, *Antiques Roadshow* (http://www.pbs.org/wgbh/pages/roadshow), where people are encouraged to bring family treasures or rummage sale bargains for appraisal by antique industry experts.

EMPLOYERS

Many antiques and art dealers and are self-employed, operating their own shops or renting space at a local mall. Others operate solely through traveling art shows or through mail-order catalogs. Some dealers prefer to work as employees of larger antique or art galleries. In general, the more well-known the dealer, the more permanent and steady the business. Prestigious auction houses such as Christie's or Sotheby's are attractive places to work, but competition for such jobs is fierce.

STARTING OUT

All dealers have a great interest in antiques or art and are collectors themselves. Often, their businesses result from an overabundance of their personal collections. There are many ways to build your collection and create inventory worthy of an antique business. Attending yard sales is an inexpensive way to build your inventory; you'll never know what kind of valuables you will come across. Flea markets, local art galleries, and antique malls will provide great purchasing opportunities and give you the chance to check out the competition. Sandra Naujokas finds that spring is an especially busy time for collecting. As people do their "spring cleaning," many decide to part with household items and décor they no longer want or need.

ADVANCEMENT

For those working out of their homes or renting showcase space at malls or larger shops, advancement in this field can mean opening their own antique shop or art gallery. Besides a business license, dealers who open their own stores need to apply for a seller's permit and a state tax identification number.

At this point, advancement is based on the success of the business. To ensure that their business thrives and expands, dealers need to develop advertising and marketing ideas to keep their business in the public's eye. Besides using the local library or Internet for ideas on opening their own businesses, newer dealers often turn to people who are already in the antiques and art business for valuable advice.

EARNINGS

It is difficult to gauge what antiques and art dealers earn because of the vastness of the industry. Some internationally known, high-end antique stores and art galleries dealing with many pieces of priceless furniture or works of art may make millions of dollars in yearly profits. This, however, is the exception. It is impossible to compare the high-end dealer with the lower end market. The majority of antiques and art dealers are comparatively small in size and type of inventory. Some dealers work only part time or rent showcase space from established shops.

According to a survey conducted by the Antiques and Collectibles National Association, the average showcase dealer earns about $1,000 a month in gross profits. From there, each dealer earns a net profit as determined by the piece or pieces sold, after overhead and other business costs. Note that annual earnings vary greatly for antiques and art dealers due to factors such as size and specialization of the store, location, the market, and current trends and tastes of the public.

WORK ENVIRONMENT

Much of antiques and art dealers' time is spent indoors. Many smaller antique shops and art galleries do not operate with a large staff, so dealers must be prepared to work alone at times. Also, there may be large gaps of time between customers. Most stores are open at least five days a week and operate during regular business hours, though some have extended shopping hours in the evening.

However, dealers are not always stuck in their store. Buying trips and shopping expeditions give them opportunities to restock their inventory, not to mention explore different regions of the country or world. Naujokas finds that spring is the busiest time for building her store's merchandise, while the holiday season is a busy selling time.

OUTLOOK

According to the Antiques and Collectibles National Association, the collectibles industry should enjoy moderate growth in future years. The Internet has quickly become a popular way to buy and sell antiques and art. Though this medium has introduced collecting to many people worldwide, it has also had an adverse affect on the industry, namely for dealers and businesses that sell antiques and art in more traditional settings such as a shop or mall, or at a trade show. However, some industry experts predict that the popularity of Web sites devoted to selling collectibles will level off. There is a great social aspect to collecting art and antiques. They believe that people want to see, feel, and touch the items they are interested in purchasing, which is obviously not possible to do while surfing the Web.

Though the number of authentic antique art and collectibles—items more than 100 years old—is limited, new items will be in vogue as collectibles. Also, people will be ready to sell old furniture and other belongings to make room for new, modern purchases. It is unlikely that there will ever be a shortage of inventory worthy of an antique shop or art gallery.

FOR MORE INFORMATION

For industry information, antique show schedules, and appraisal information, contact
Antiques and Collectibles National Association
PO Box 4389
Davidson, NC 28036-4389
Tel: 800-287-7127
http://www.antiqueandcollectible.com

For art resources and listings of galleries, contact
Art Dealers Association of America
575 Madison Avenue
New York, NY 10022-2511
Tel: 212-940-8590
http://www.artdealers.org

Contact the FADA for information on art galleries nationwide and special events.
Fine Art Dealers Association (FADA)
PO Box D1
Carmel By the Sea, CA 93921-0729
http://www.fada.com

For information about appraising and certification, contact
International Society of Appraisers
1131 SW Seventh Street, Suite 105
Renton, WA 98057-1215
Tel: 206-241-0359
Email: isa@isa-appraisers.org
http://www.isa-appraisers.org

For programming schedules and tour information on the public television show that highlights unique and sometimes priceless antique finds, visit
Antiques Roadshow
http://www.pbs.org/wgbh/pages/roadshow

For information on collecting, art and antique shows, and collecting clubs, visit
Collectors.org
http://www.collectors.org

Art Directors

OVERVIEW

Art directors play a key role in every stage of the creation of an advertisement or ad campaign, from formulating concepts to supervising production. Ultimately, they are responsible for planning and overseeing the presentation of their clients' messages in print or on-screen—that is, in books, magazines, newspapers, television commercials, posters, and packaging, as well as in film and video and on the Internet.

In publishing, art directors work with artists, photographers, and text editors to develop visual images and generate copy, according to the marketing strategy. They are responsible for evaluating existing illustrations, determining presentation styles and techniques, hiring both staff and freelance talent, working with layouts, and preparing budgets.

In films, videos, and television commercials, art directors set the general look of the visual elements and approve the props, costumes, and models. In addition, they are involved in casting, editing, and selecting the music. In film (motion pictures) and video, the art director is usually an experienced animator or computer/graphic arts designer who supervises animators or other artistic staff.

In sum, art directors are charged with selling to, informing, and educating consumers. They supervise both in-house and off-site staff, handle executive issues, and oversee the entire artistic production process. There are approximately 71,000 art directors working in the United States.

QUICK FACTS

School Subjects
Art
Business
Computer science

Personal Skills
Artistic
Communication/ideas

Work Environment
Primarily indoors
Primarily one location

Minimum Education Level
Bachelor's degree

Salary Range
$37,920 to $68,100 to $135,090+

Certification or Licensing
None available

Outlook
About as fast as the average

DOT
164

GOE
01.01.01

NOC
5131

O*NET-SOC
27-1011.00

HISTORY

Artists have always been an important part of the creative process throughout history. Medieval monks illuminated their manuscripts, painting with egg-white tempera on vellum. Each copy of each book had to be printed and illustrated individually.

Printed illustrations first appeared in books in 1461. Through the years, prints were made through woodblock, copperplate, lithography, and other means of duplicating images. Although making many copies of the same illustration was now possible, publishers still depended on individual artists to create the original works. Text editors usually decided what was to be illustrated and how, while artists commonly supervised the production of the artwork.

The first art directors were probably staff illustrators for book publishers. As the publishing industry grew more complex and incorporated new technologies such as photography and film, art direction evolved into a more supervisory position and became a full-time job. Publishers and advertisers began to need specialists who could acquire and use illustrations and photos. Women's magazines, such as *Vogue* (http://www.style.com/vogue) and *Harper's Bazaar* (http://www.harpersbazaar.com), and photo magazines, such as *National Geographic* (http://www.nationalgeographic.com), relied so much on illustration and photography that the photo editor and art director began to carry as much power as the text editor.

With the creation of animation, art directors became more indispensable than ever. Animated short films, such as the early Mickey Mouse cartoons, were usually supervised by art directors. Walt Disney, himself, was the art director on many of his early pictures. And as full-length films have moved into animation, the sheer number of illustrations requires more than one art director to oversee the project.

Today's art directors supervise almost every type of visual project produced. Through a variety of methods and media, from television and film to magazines, comic books, and the Internet, art directors communicate ideas by selecting and supervising every element that goes into the finished product.

THE JOB

Art directors are responsible for all visual aspects of printed or on-screen projects. The art director oversees the process of developing visual solutions to a variety of communication problems. He or she helps to establish corporate identities; advertises products and services; enhances books, magazines, newsletters, and other publications; and creates television commercials, film and video productions, and Web sites. Some art directors with experience or knowledge in specific fields specialize in such areas as packaging, exhibitions and displays, or the Internet. But all directors, even those with specialized backgrounds, must be skilled in and knowledgeable about design, illustration, photography, computers, research, and writing in order to supervise the work of graphic artists, photographers, copywriters, text editors, and other employees.

In print advertising and publishing, art directors may begin with the client's concept or develop one in collaboration with the copywriter and account executive. Once the concept is established, the next step is to decide on the most effective way to communicate it. If there is text, for example, should the art director choose illustrations based on specific text references, or should the illustrations fill in the gaps in the copy? If a piece is being revised, existing illustrations must be reevaluated.

After deciding what needs to be illustrated, art directors must find sources that can create or provide the art. Photo agencies, for example, have photographs and illustrations on thousands of different subjects. If, however, the desired illustration does not exist, it may have to be commissioned or designed by one of the staff designers. Commissioning artwork means that the art director contacts a photographer or illustrator and explains what is needed. A price is negotiated, and the artist creates the image specifically for the art director.

Once the illustrations and other art elements have been secured, they must be presented in an appealing manner. The art director supervises (and may help in the production of) the layout of the piece and presents the final version to the client or creative director. Layout is the process of figuring out where every image, headline, and block of text will be placed on the page. The size, style, and method of reproduction must all be specifically indicated so that the image is re-created as the director intended it.

In broadcast advertising and film and video, the art director has a wide variety of responsibilities and often interacts with an enormous number of creative professionals. Working with directors and producers, art directors interpret scripts and create or select settings in order to visually convey the story or the message. The art director oversees and channels the talents of set decorators and designers, model makers, location managers, propmasters, construction coordinators, and special effects people. In addition, art directors work with writers, unit production managers, cinematographers, costume designers, and post-production staff, including editors and employees responsible for scoring and titles. The art director is ultimately responsible for all visual aspects of the finished product.

The process of producing a television commercial begins in much the same way that a printed advertising piece is created. The art director may start with the client's concept or create one in-house in collaboration with staff members. Once a concept has been created and the copywriter has generated the corresponding text, the art director sketches a rough storyboard based on the writer's ideas, and the plan is presented for review to the creative director. The next step is to develop a finished storyboard, with larger and more detailed frames (the individual scenes) in color. This storyboard is presented to the client for review and used as a guide for the film director as well.

Technology has been playing an increasingly important role in the art director's job. Most art directors, for example, use a variety of computer software programs, including Adobe InDesign, Frame-Maker, Illustrator, and Photoshop; Macromedia Dreamweaver; QuarkXPress; and CorelDRAW. Many others create and oversee Web sites for clients and work with other interactive media and materials, including CD-ROM, touch screens, multidimensional visuals, and new animation programs.

Art directors usually work on more than one project at a time and must be able to keep numerous, unrelated details straight. They often work under pressure of a deadline and yet must remain calm and pleasant when dealing with clients and staff. Because they are supervisors, art directors are often called upon to resolve problems, not only with projects but with employees as well.

Art directors are not entry-level workers. They usually have years of experience working at lower-level jobs in the field before gaining the knowledge needed to supervise projects. Depending on whether they work primarily in publishing or film, art directors have to know how printing presses operate or how film is processed. They should also be familiar with a variety of production techniques in order to understand the wide range of ways that images can be manipulated to meet the needs of a project.

REQUIREMENTS

High School

A college degree is usually a requirement for art directors; however, in some instances, it is not absolutely necessary. A variety of high school courses will give you both a taste of college-level offerings and an idea of the skills necessary for art directors on the job. These courses include art, drawing, art history, graphic design, illustration, photography, advertising, and desktop publishing.

Math courses are also important. Most of the elements of sizing an image involve calculating percentage reduction or enlargement of the original picture. This must be done with a great degree of accuracy if the overall design is going to work. For example, type size may have to be figured within a thirty-second of an inch for a print project. Errors can be extremely costly and may make the project look sloppy.

Other useful courses that you should take in high school include business, computing, English, technical drawing, cultural studies, psychology, and social science.

Postsecondary Training

According to the American Institute of Graphic Arts, nine out of 10 artists have a college degree. Among them, six out of 10 have majored in graphic design, and two out of 10 have majored in fine arts. In addition, almost two out of 10 have a master's degree. Along with general two- and four-year colleges and universities, a number of professional art schools offer two-, three-, or four-year programs with such classes as figure drawing, painting, graphic design, and other art courses, as well as classes in art history, writing, business administration, communications, and foreign languages.

Courses in advertising, marketing, photography, filmmaking, set direction, layout, desktop publishing, and fashion are also important for those interested in becoming art directors. Specialized courses, sometimes offered only at professional art schools, may be particularly helpful for students who want to go into art direction. These include typography, animation, storyboard, Web site design, and portfolio development.

Because of the rapidly increasing use of computers in design work, it is essential to have a thorough understanding of how computer art and layout programs work. In smaller companies, the art director may be responsible for operating this equipment; in larger companies, a staff person, under the direction of the art director, may use these programs. In either case, the director must know what can be done with the available equipment.

In addition to course work at the college level, many universities and professional art schools offer graduates or students in their final year a variety of workshop projects, desktop publishing training opportunities, and internships. These programs provide students with opportunities to develop their personal design styles as well as their portfolios.

Other Requirements

The work of an art director requires creativity, imagination, curiosity, and a sense of adventure. Art directors must be able to work with all sorts of specialized equipment and computer software, such as graphic design programs, as well as make presentations on the ideas behind their work.

The ability to work well with different people and organizations is a must for art directors. They must always be up-to-date on new techniques, trends, and attitudes. And because deadlines are a constant part of the work, an ability to handle stress and pressure well is key.

Accuracy and attention to detail are important parts of the job. When art is done neatly and correctly, the public usually pays no notice. But when a project is done poorly or sloppily, people will notice, even if they have had no design training. Other requirements for art directors include time management skills and an interest in media and people's motivations and lifestyles.

EXPLORING

High school students can get an idea of what an art director does by working on the staff of the school newspaper, magazine, or yearbook, and developing their own Web sites or zines. It may also be possible to secure a part-time job assisting the advertising director of the local newspaper or to work at an advertising agency. Developing your own artistic talent is important, and this can be accomplished through self-training (reading books and practicing) or through courses in painting, drawing, or other creative arts. At the very least, you should develop your "creative eye"; that is, your ability to develop ideas visually. One way to do this is by familiarizing yourself with great works, such as paintings or highly creative magazine ads, motion pictures, videos, or commercials.

Students can also become members of a variety of art or advertising clubs around the nation. If you have access to the Internet, check out Paleta: The Art Project (http://www.paletaworld.org) to join a free art club. In addition to keeping members up to date on industry trends, such clubs offer job information, resources, and many other benefits.

EMPLOYERS

A variety of organizations in virtually all industries employ art directors. They might work at advertising agencies, publishing houses, museums, packaging firms, photography studios, marketing and public relations firms, desktop publishing outfits, digital prepress houses, or printing companies. Art directors who oversee and produce on-screen products often work for film production houses, Web designers, multimedia developers, computer games developers, or television stations.

While companies of all sizes employ art directors, smaller organizations often combine the positions of graphic designer, illustrator, and art director. And although opportunities for art direction can be found all across the nation and abroad, many larger firms in such cities as Chicago, New York, and Los Angeles usually have more openings, as well as higher pay scales, than smaller companies.

STARTING OUT

Since an art director's job requires a great deal of experience, it is usually not considered an entry-level position. Typically, a person on a career track toward art director is hired as an assistant to an established director. Recent graduates wishing to enter advertising should have a portfolio of their work containing seven to 10 sample ads to demonstrate their understanding of both the business and the media in which they want to work.

Mean Earnings by Industry, 2006

Management of companies and enterprises	$92,830
Specialized design services	$90,030
Motion picture and video industries	$88,390
Advertising and related services	$82,680
Newspaper, periodical, book, and directory publishers	$65,800

Source: U.S. Department of Labor

Serving as an intern is a good way to get experience and develop skills. Graduates should also consider taking an entry-level job in a publisher's art department to gain initial experience. Either way, aspiring art directors must be willing to acquire their credentials by working on various projects. This may mean working in a variety of areas, such as advertising, marketing, editing, and design.

College publications offer students a chance to gain experience and develop portfolios. In addition, many students are able to do freelance work while still in school, allowing them to make important industry contacts and gain on-the-job experience at the same time.

ADVANCEMENT

While some may be content upon reaching the position of art director to remain there, many art directors take on even more responsibility within their organizations, become television directors, start their own advertising agencies, create their own Web sites, develop original multimedia programs, or launch their own magazines.

Many people who get to the position of art director do not advance beyond the title but move on to work at more prestigious firms. Competition for positions at companies that have national reputations continues to be keen because of the sheer number of talented people interested. At smaller publications or local companies, the competition may be less intense, since candidates are competing primarily against others in the local market.

EARNINGS

The job title of art director can mean many different things, depending on the company at which the director is employed. According to the U.S. Department of Labor, a beginning art director or an art director who worked at a small firm earned $37,920 or less per year in 2006, while experienced art directors working at larger companies earned more than $135,090. Mean annual earnings for art directors employed in the advertising industry (the largest employer of salaried art directors) were $82,680 in 2006. The median annual earnings for art directors working in all industries were $68,100. (Again, it is important to note that these positions are not entry level; beginning art directors have probably already accumulated several years of experience in the field for which they were paid far less.)

According to the American Institute of Graphic Arts/Aquent Salary Survey 2007, the median salary for art directors was $70,000. Art directors in the 25th percentile earned $55,000 annually, while those in the 75th percentile made $82,000 per year. Salaries varied by geographic region. For example, art directors in the Mid-Atlantic states had average salaries of $75,000 a year, while those in the Mountain region earned an average of $55,000.

Most companies employing art directors offer insurance benefits, a retirement plan, and other incentives and bonuses.

WORK ENVIRONMENT

Art directors usually work in studios or office buildings. While their work areas are ordinarily comfortable, well lit, and ventilated, they often handle glue, paint, ink, and other materials that pose safety hazards, and they should, therefore, exercise caution.

Art directors at art and design studios and publishing firms usually work a standard 40-hour week. Many, however, work overtime during busy periods to meet deadlines. Similarly, directors at film and video operations and at television studios work as many hours as required—usually many more than 40 per week—in order to finish projects according to predetermined schedules.

While art directors work independently when reviewing artwork and reading copy, much of their time is spent collaborating with and supervising a team of employees, often consisting of copywriters, editors, photographers, graphic artists, and account executives.

OUTLOOK

The extent to which art director positions are in demand, like many other positions, depends on the economy in general; when times are tough, people and businesses spend less, and cutbacks are made. When the economy is healthy, employment prospects for art directors will be favorable. The U.S. Department of Labor predicts that employment for art directors will grow about as fast as the average for all other occupations through 2014. One area that shows particularly good promise for growth is the retail industry, since more and more large retail establishments, especially catalog houses, will be employing in-house advertising art directors.

In addition, producers of all kinds of products continually need advertisers to reach their potential customers, and publishers always want some type of illustration to enhance their books and magazines. Creators of films and videos also need images to produce their programs, and people working with new media are increasingly looking for artists and directors to promote new and existing products and services, enhance their Web sites, develop new multimedia programs, and create multidimensional visuals. People who can quickly and creatively generate new concepts and ideas will be in high demand.

However, it is important to note that the supply of aspiring artists is expected to exceed the number of job openings. As a result, those wishing to enter the field will encounter keen competition for salaried, staff positions as well as for freelance work. And although the Internet is expected to provide many opportunities for artists and art directors, some firms are hiring employees without formal art or design training to operate computer-aided design systems and oversee work.

FOR MORE INFORMATION

The AAF is the professional advertising association that binds the mutual interests of corporate advertisers, agencies, media companies, suppliers, and academia. For more information, contact
American Advertising Federation (AAF)
1101 Vermont Avenue, NW, Suite 500
Washington, DC 20005-6306
Tel: 800-999-2231
Email: aaf@aaf.org
http://www.aaf.org

This management-oriented national trade organization represents the advertising agency business. For information, contact
American Association of Advertising Agencies
405 Lexington Avenue, 18th Floor
New York, NY 10174-1801
Tel: 212-682-2500
http://www.aaaa.org

For more information on design professionals, contact
American Institute of Graphic Arts
164 Fifth Avenue
New York, NY 10010-5901
Tel: 212-807-1990
http://www.aiga.org

The Art Directors Club is an international, nonprofit organization of directors in advertising, graphic design, interactive media, broadcast design, typography, packaging, environmental design, photography, illustration, and related disciplines. For information, contact

Art Directors Club
106 West 29th Street
New York, NY 10001-5301
Tel: 212-643-1440
Email: info@adcglobal.org
http://www.adcglobal.org

Art Teachers

OVERVIEW

Art teachers instruct students how to produce, appreciate, and understand the fine arts. Like teachers in other fields, they develop teaching outlines and lesson plans, give lectures, facilitate discussions and activities, keep class attendance records, assign homework, and evaluate student progress. *Elementary school art teachers* instruct younger students in the fundamentals of art, such as colors and basic drawing, while *secondary school art teachers* and *college art professors* generally specialize in one area of art, such as studio art, photography, ceramics, or computer imaging. This article will focus on art teachers at the elementary and secondary levels, as well as those who teach self-enrichment classes at private educational institutions and other settings. See the article College Professors, Art, for information on art teachers at the postsecondary level.

HISTORY

Early art training for children in the United States largely consisted of the informal education of "girls in the ornamental arts and boys in drawing and architecture," according to *A History of Art Education,* a Web site developed by art education graduate students at the University of North Texas.

Many early attempts at art education focused on instruction in drawing. The first drawing class was offered at Central High School in Pittsburg, Pennsylvania, in 1840. It was taught by Rembrandt Peale, a well-known artist who is best known today for his portraits of George Washington and Thomas Jefferson. In 1870, the Massachusetts Drawing Act was passed in response to public concern that the United States was relying too much on imports and was producing no goods of its own that could be used or sold. The act required the introduction of industrial drawing instruction by Massachusetts public schools in towns whose population exceeded 10,000. Soon after, Maine, New York, and Vermont enacted similar laws. The implementation of these laws created an immediate need for qualified instructors and training programs. In 1873, the Massachusetts Normal Art School (known as the Massachusetts College of Art today) was established to prepare teachers of drawing.

In the following decades, art education in elementary and secondary schools continued to grow in popularity.

The National Art Education Association was formed in 1947 to represent the professional interests of art educators. It had 3,500 members at its formation. Today, it has approximately 22,000 members. One of the association's most important accomplishments was the introduction of the National Visual Arts Standards in 1994. The standards for K-12 education provide "guidelines for visual art programs, instruction, and teacher training and state what students should know and do in the arts."

THE JOB

Art teachers work in schools, community centers, and museums around the country. Much of the details about their job depends on the age level for which they teach.

In the first and second grades, art teachers cover the basic art skills: drawing, coloring, and identifying pictures and colors. With older students, teachers may introduce new materials and art procedures, such as sketching still life or working with papier-mâché. To capture attention and teach new concepts, they use arts and crafts projects and other interactive activities. Although they are usually required to follow a curriculum designed by state or local administrators, teachers study new learning methods to incorporate into the classroom, such as using computers to create and manipulate artwork.

Secondary school art teachers teach students more advanced art concepts, such as ceramics and photography, in addition to basic studio art. Though secondary teachers are likely to be assigned to one specific grade level, they may be required to teach students in surrounding grades. For example, a secondary school art teacher may teach illustration to a class of ninth graders one period and advanced photography to high school seniors the next.

Art teachers must have a strong love of art and enjoy teaching others about the field. *(Jeff Greenberg, The Image Works)*

In the classroom, secondary school art teachers rely on a variety of teaching methods. Because their students are more mature, they often integrate lectures about artists, procedures, and art history in with studio time. This lecture time also may include opportunities for student discussion about famous works and their own artwork. Secondary art teachers may also show films and videos, use computers and the Internet, bring in guest speakers, and organize field trips to enhance learning and keep students engaged in the subject.

Some art educators teach art at community centers, day care centers, juvenile detention centers, and other nonacademic settings. They might teach beginning drawing to a group of eight-year-olds, ceramics to high school students, or an advanced digital photography class to adults. Art teachers who work in these settings typically work part time, although some full-time positions are available.

All art teachers devote a fair amount of time to preparation outside of the classroom. They prepare daily lesson plans and assignments, grade papers, tests, and artwork, and keep a record of each student's progress. Other responsibilities include communicating with parents, advisers, or students through written reports and scheduled meetings, ordering art supplies, keeping their classroom orderly, and decorating desks and bulletin boards to keep the learning environment visually stimulating. They also continue to study alternative and traditional teaching methods, as well as art techniques, to hone their skills.

Most elementary and secondary art teachers are contracted to work 10 months out of the year, with a two-month vacation during the summer. During their summer break, many continue their education to renew or upgrade their teaching licenses and earn higher salaries. Teachers in schools that operate year-round work eight-week sessions with one-week breaks in between and a five-week vacation in the winter.

REQUIREMENTS

High School

To prepare for a career in art education, follow your school's college preparatory program and take advanced courses in English, mathematics, science, history, and government—in addition to art. Composition, journalism, and communications classes are also important for developing your writing and speaking skills.

Postsecondary Training

Your college training will depend on the level at which you plan to teach. All 50 states and the District of Columbia require public elementary education teachers to have a bachelor's degree in either education or in the subject they teach. Prospective teachers must also complete an approved training program, which combines subject and educational classes with work experience in the classroom, called student teaching.

If you want to teach at the high school level, you may choose to major in art while taking required education courses, or you may major in secondary education with a concentration in art. Similar to prospective elementary teachers, you will need to student teach in an actual classroom environment.

Certification and Licensing

Elementary and secondary art teachers who work in public schools must be licensed under regulations established by the state in which they teach. If they move to another state, teachers have to comply with any other regulations in their new state to be able to teach there, though many states have reciprocity agreements, which means they accept out-of-state licensure, that make it easier for teachers to change locations.

To become licensed, prospective art teachers must be knowledgeable of several art subjects and complete an approved teaching program with the appropriate course credits in both education and art and a period of student teaching. Many states are moving toward a performance-based evaluation for licensing. In this case, after passing the teaching examination, prospective teachers are given provisional licenses. Only after proving themselves capable in the classroom are they eligible for a full license.

Other Requirements

Many consider the desire to teach a calling. This calling is based on a love of learning. Teachers of young children and young adults must respect their students as individuals, with personalities, strengths, and weaknesses of their own. They must also be patient and self-disciplined to manage a large group independently. Because they work with students who are at very impressionable ages, they should serve as good role models. Elementary and secondary teachers should also be well organized, as they have to keep track of the work and progress of a number of different students. In addition, they should be creative, have artistic ability, and have a strong love of art and teaching others about the field.

EXPLORING

Talk to your art teachers about their careers. Ask them what they like and dislike about the career, what they studied in college, and how they landed their first job, among other questions. You can develop your own teaching experience by volunteering at a community center that offers art classes or working at a summer art camp. And, of course, take as many art classes as you possibly can.

EMPLOYERS

Art teachers work at public and private institutions, museums, day care centers, juvenile detention centers, community centers, and schools of the arts. Although rural areas maintain schools, more teaching positions are available in urban or suburban areas. Art teachers also find opportunities in charter schools, which are smaller, deregulated schools that receive public funding.

STARTING OUT

After completing the teacher certification process, including your months of student teaching, you'll work with your college's career services office to find a full-time position. The departments of education of some states maintain listings of job openings. Many schools advertise teaching positions in the classifieds of the state's major newspapers. You may also directly contact the principals and superintendents of the schools in which you'd like to work. While waiting for full-time work, you can work as a substitute teacher. In urban areas with many schools, you may be able to substitute full time.

ADVANCEMENT

As elementary and secondary art teachers acquire experience or additional education, they can expect higher wages and more responsibilities. Teachers with leadership skills and an interest in administrative work may advance to serve as principals or supervisors, though the number of these positions is limited and competition is fierce. Another move may be into higher education, teaching art classes at a college or university. For most of these positions, additional education is required. Other common career transitions

Books to Read: Modern Art Movements

Batchelor, David. *Minimalism*. New York: Cambridge University Press, 1997.

Behr, Shulamith. *Expressionism*. New York: Cambridge University Press, 2000.

Caws, Mary Ann. *Surrealism*. Boston: Phaidon Press, 2004.

Cottington, David. *Cubism and Its Histories*. Manchester, U.K.: Manchester University Press, 2005.

Foster, Hal, Rosalind Krauss, Yve-Alain Bois, and Benjamin Buchloh. *Art Since 1900: Modernism, Antimodernism, Postmodernism*. New York: Thames & Hudson, 2005.

Ganz, Nicholas. *Graffiti World: Street Art from Five Continents*. New York: Harry N. Abrams, 2004.

Harrison, Charles. *Modernism*. New York: Cambridge University Press, 1998.

Heartney, Eleanor. *Postmodernism*. New York: Cambridge University Press, 2001.

Humphreys, Richard. *Futurism*. New York: Cambridge University Press, 1999.

Hunter, Sam, Daniel Wheeler, and John M. Jacobus. *Modern Art: Painting, Sculpture, Architecture*. 3d ed. New York: Prentice Hall, 2000.

Thomson, Belinda. *Impressionism: Origins, Practice, Reception*. New York: Thames & Hudson, 2000.

Thomson, Belinda. *Post-Impressionism*. New York: Cambridge University Press, 1998.

are into the business world, such as moving to advertising, graphic design, or other related field.

EARNINGS

According to the U.S. Department of Labor, the median annual salary for elementary school teachers was $45,570 in 2006. The lowest paid 10 percent earned $30,370 or less; the highest paid 10 percent earned $72,720 or more. The median annual salary for secondary school teachers was $47,740 in 2006. Salaries ranged from less than $31,760 to $76,100 or more annually.

Self-enrichment education teachers (including those who teach art) earned median annual salaries of $33,440 in 2006. Salaries ranged from less than $17,740 to $66,600 or more annually.

Benefits for art teachers who are employed by schools typically include health insurance, sick pay, 401(k) plans, and reimbursement for continuing education.

WORK ENVIRONMENT

Art teachers work in generally pleasant conditions, although some older schools may have poor heating or electrical systems. The work can seem confining, requiring them to remain in the classroom throughout most of the day. Elementary school art teachers have to deal with busy children all day, which can be tiring and trying.

Elementary and high school hours are generally 8 a.m. to 3 p.m., but art teachers work more than 40 hours a week teaching, preparing for classes, grading papers and artwork, and directing extracurricular activities.

OUTLOOK

According to the *Occupational Outlook Handbook,* employment opportunities for teachers (grades K–12) are expected to grow as fast as the average for all occupations through 2014. The need to replace retiring teachers will provide many opportunities nationwide. However, the demand for art teachers will be much lower, because schools hire a limited number of art faculty. Additionally, there is a surplus of talented, qualified art professionals wanting to get into teaching. Positions in inner-city schools or rural areas may be easier to find. Art teachers who teach self-enrichment classes at private educational institutions and in other settings should have slightly better employment opportunities—although these positions are typically part time and offer lower salaries than positions in formal school settings.

FOR MORE INFORMATION

For information about union membership, contact

American Federation of Teachers
555 New Jersey Avenue, NW
Washington, DC 20001-2029
Tel: 202-879-4400
http://www.aft.org

For information on student membership and useful publications, contact

National Art Education Association
1916 Association Drive
Reston, VA 20191-1590
Tel: 703-860-8000
Email: info@naea-reston.org
http://www.naea-reston.org

For information on accredited teacher education programs and teaching careers, contact

National Council for Accreditation of Teacher Education
2010 Massachusetts Avenue, NW, Suite 500
Washington, DC 20036-1023
Tel: 202-466-7496
http://www.ncate.org

Book Conservators

QUICK FACTS

School Subjects
Art
History

Personal Skills
Artistic
Mechanical/manipulative

Work Environment
Primarily indoors
Primarily one location

Minimum Education Level
Bachelor's degree

Salary Range
$20,600 to $34,340 to
$61,270+

Certification or Licensing
Voluntary

Outlook
About as fast as the average

DOT
102

GOE
12.03.04

NOC
5112

O*NET-SOC
25-4013.00

OVERVIEW

Book conservators treat the bindings and pages of books and other objects to help preserve original materials for future use. Their work often includes removing a book block from its binding, sewing, measuring, gluing, rebinding, and using special chemical treatments to maintain the integrity of the item. Most conservators work in libraries, in museums, or for special conservation centers.

HISTORY

In order to understand the history of book conservation as a field, it is important to learn about the evolution of books and bookbinding. Early books were not bound, but rather rolled, such as ancient Egyptian papyrus rolls and early Christian parchment rolls. Eventually the rolls were cut into a number of flat panels sewn together along one edge, thus allowing for a book that was more convenient, portable, and enduring. Early Latin codex manuscripts were made up of folded sheets gathered into signatures, or groups of folded pages, and sewn together. Wooden boards were then placed on either side of the sewn signatures. In time, the entire volume was covered with leather or other animal skins to hide the sewing cords and provide protection to the pages. The basic constructional elements of bookbinding have changed little in the past 1,800 years, but the materials and methods used have matured considerably.

Before the invention of the printing press, religious orders were often charged with copying texts by hand. These same monastic groups also assumed the roles of bookbinder and conservator. One of the main goals in creating books is the conservation and dissemination of knowledge.

In order to pass that knowledge on to future generations, many early bookbinders began the legacy of conservation by using high-quality materials and excellent craftsmanship. A book that is well crafted in the first place will need less invasive conservation as the material ages. Historically, then, those who created the books had the specialized knowledge to conserve them.

Conservators today are often from the same mold as early bookbinders. They have the specialized knowledge of how books have traditionally been crafted, and they use technologically advanced adhesives, papers, and binding techniques to ensure that materials created centuries ago will be around for years to come.

The establishment of book conservation as a career field apart from bookbinding probably began when the first courses in conservation and preservation were taught at a library school, or when a professional library association first addressed the topic. Thus, although early bookbinders dealt with issues of material longevity, conservation as a field has only been around for 100 years or so.

THE JOB

Book conservators work to slow down or stabilize the deterioration of books and other print-based materials. They repair books that have been damaged by misuse, accident, pests, or normal wear and tear; treat items that may have been produced or repaired with inferior materials or methods; and work to ensure that the books will be around for the future.

Before beginning any conservation efforts, book conservators must examine the item to be restored, determine the extent and cause of the deterioration, evaluate their own conservation skills, and decide on a proper course of action. In deciding how to treat an item, the book conservator must first consider the history of the item. When was it made? Book conservators must have a good knowledge of the history of bookmaking in order to serve the needs of the item. A book bound by hand in Italy in 1600 will have different needs than a volume bound by machine in 1980.

The book conservator also needs to consider what other repairs have been made to the book over the years. Sometimes a shoddy repair job in the past can create more work for today's conservator. For example, someone 30 years ago may have taped a torn page to keep it from ripping out entirely. Unfortunately, this hasty action, coupled with tape that will not stand the test of time, could lead to cracked, yellowing tape and stained book pages. When repairing a ripped sheet, book conservators use a pH-neutral (acid-free) adhesive, such as wheat paste, and Japanese paper, or a special acid-free book tape. Since high levels of acidity in papers and materials increase the rate of deterioration, all materials that conservators use must be acid-free and of archival quality.

Book conservators also think about the current and future use of the book. For a common, high-use volume that will be checked out of the library frequently, they may repair the book with cheaper, lower-quality materials that will survive being tossed into a backpack and repeated trips through the return chute. For a textbook that is reprinted each year, for example, a thick piece of tape may be an adequate conservation method. If such a book is falling out of its cover, the conservator may need to remove the bookblock entirely, repair or replace the end sheets and headbands, and re-glue the bookblock back into the cover. If the cover of the book is broken, the conservator may need to fit the text block into a new cover. This involves measuring the binder's board and book cloth, cutting the materials to size, gluing the cloth onto the board, sizing in the bookblock, then finally gluing and setting the book. After the glue is dry, the conservator will inspect the item to ensure that all materials were fitted in properly, and that all problems were corrected.

Rare books that are handled less frequently or only by specially trained and careful users can have less invasive repairs in order to maintain the integrity of the original item. For instance, a conservator may choose to make a box to house a book rather than repair a broken spine. If the conservation work would lessen the value of the book, sometimes it's better to simply stop the deterioration rather than to repair the damage.

The historical and monetary value of a book is a key factor in deciding upon treatment. As with any antique, often less restoration is more. On a recent antiques television program, an owner refinished an antique table and thereby reduced its resale value by thousands of dollars. The same can be said for books. Many old and rare books have great value because of the historical materials and methods in evidence.

Sometimes pests are encountered in conservation work. Beetle larvae and other insects may feast upon crumbs left in books, the pulp of the paper, or the adhesive, and make holes in the text. The conservator will assess the extent of the damage and prescribe a treatment. For critter damage to books, the most important thing is to ensure that any infestation is under control. The conservator needs to make sure that all bugs in a book are dead; if not, the items may need to be taken to a professional for fumigation. Once that process is complete, the conservator can look at possible repair options. If the damage is under control, the conservator will probably opt for further damage prevention in lieu of repair.

Often conservators treat books for only part of their day. They might also spend much time working on ways to minimize the need for conservation and repair work in the first place. Book conservators who work as part of a large department have other duties, such as dealing with patrons, reference work, security, training assistants, fielding calls from the public, giving seminars, and teaching. Conservators may also serve on groups and committees devoted to preservation, conservation, and the administration of a conservation lab or department.

REQUIREMENTS

High School

You should plan on taking a college preparatory course load while in high school. Classes such as history, literature, art, foreign languages, chemistry, and mathematics will help you build a strong background for book conservation. By studying history, you can learn the social and historical contexts of books and knowledge. Understanding the history of an item can give you a better perspective on approaching the material as a conservator. Strong knowledge of literature can help you appraise the potential value of a book. A comprehension of foreign languages allows you to deal with a wider variety of books from around the globe. Chemistry and math will begin to teach you about the composition and measurement of the materials you will be using. Art will teach you how to use your hands to create beautiful works that last.

Postsecondary Training

In the past, book conservators gained their training by participating in an apprenticeship or internship. Today, graduate programs in book conservation have become the primary method of training to enter this field, although some students still enter this field after earning a bachelor's degree and completing an apprenticeship or internship to round out their training. A bachelor's degree in art, art history, or one of the fine arts may help you gain entry into a book conservation apprenticeship or internship program. Your school may offer courses, or even an undergraduate degree, in the book or paper arts, which often include classes in preservation and conservation. You will also need to take courses that help you learn how to select items for conservation, how to purchase and best utilize your conservation materials, and how to prepare documentation on your conservation methods and treatments.

Upon earning a bachelor's degree, you should attend a graduate school that offers training in book conservation. These programs are commonly offered by the art conservation departments of academic institutions. Some students may wish to earn a master's degree in library science with a concentration in book and document conservation. Again, advanced degrees may not be necessary for some positions, but they can always help you gain more prominent positions—particularly in administration—and perhaps command a higher salary. Additionally, any special skills you gain through advanced education will make you more attractive to potential employers and private clients.

Certification or Licensing
Some book conservators gain certification from professional organizations such as the Academy of Certified Archivists. The certification process generally requires a mix of formal study of theory and practice, as well as a certain amount of actual experience in the field. Certification is not officially required by any federal, state, or local agencies, but some employers may request, or require, a certified book conservationist for particular positions or projects. Also, certifying organizations compile a list of all their certified conservators. If someone contacts an organization looking for a conservator, the agency will refer the client to member book conservators in the area.

Other Requirements
Book conservators need be able to think creatively. Conservation projects require the conservator to visualize the end product before beginning work. Conservators should enjoy problem solving and be able to decide the best way to conserve the materials. Having a knack for hands-on work is key as well, since book conservators spend a majority of their time inspecting materials and making repairs by hand.

Since book conservators routinely work with musty, moldy, and mildewed books, they should not be overly sensitive to odors. They also deal with sharp instruments, such as awls, knives, and paper cutters, so for safety reasons they should have a certain amount of facility with their hands. Book conservators also work with adhesives and chemicals, so they must take care not to spill materials.

Although much of their day is spent working with books, many conservators deal with the public as well. Book conservators, therefore, should be able to communicate well, and with a certain measure of tact, with many types of people. They should be able to explain conservation options to clients and to best determine what procedures will meet the needs of the material and the owner.

EXPLORING

If you are interested in becoming a book conservator, you should start out by learning all you can about how books are made. Study the history of books and of binding. Purchase an inexpensive, hardcover book at a used bookstore and take it apart to see how the bookblock is sewn together and how it is connected to the cover. Then try to put the book back together. There are many "how to" bookbinding guides to help you. Check out *Hand Bookbinding: A Manual of Instruction* by Aldren A. Watson (New York: Dover Publications, 1996) or *ABC of Bookbinding: A Unique Glossary With Over 700 Illustrations for Collectors & Librarians* by Jane Greenfield (New Castle, Del.: Oak Knoll Books, 2002) for the history of different styles of bookbinding and definitions of terms used in the field.

Contact the conservation or preservation department at your local library. The department may offer tours of its facilities or workshops on the proper care of books. Contact professional librarian associations; they may have divisions devoted to conservation. Community colleges and art museums often have weekend or evening classes in the conservation and book arts.

Finally, you might try contacting your local park district or community center to suggest sessions about book conservation. Many such groups offer summer day camps or after-school programs and look for input from participants about what types of activities are of interest. Plus, if you have had some conservation experience of your own, you could offer to teach younger students about how they can begin conserving books by taking good care of their own materials and the books they check out of the library.

EMPLOYERS

College and university libraries, public libraries, institutional libraries, and special libraries all employ book conservators. These organizations may have an entire department devoted to the conservation and preservation of materials, or the tasks of conservation may be bestowed upon another division, such as an archival or rare book collection. Museums sometimes have a specific book conservator post, or they may offer such duties to an interested art conservationist. Book conservators also work for companies devoted to material conservation. Binderies may hire a conservationist as a quality control consultant.

Some book conservators are self-employed, working on a freelance or part-time basis for organizations and private citizens. They may be part of a nationwide network of certified book conservators. Often, potential clients contact book conservators through membership in professional organizations.

STARTING OUT

Book conservation is a field that relies heavily on skill, reputation, and word-of-mouth communication. While earning your bachelor's or master's degree, you should try to get an internship, apprenticeship, or assistantship in conservation or a related field. Take all the courses you can that will help you gain conservation skills.

You may also be able to get a part-time or summer job in your school library's preservation or conservation department. Many part-time positions or internships can turn into full-time jobs after the incumbent has proven his or her skills or completed specific educational requirements.

Once you complete a training period, you might consider becoming certified. Certification can be a deciding factor in gaining employment, since certain companies and organizations may require book conservators to have official affirmation of their qualifications from an outside agency.

You should also join a conservator's organization in order to get to know professionals in the field. Since many conservator positions are in libraries, you may wish to join a professional library association as well. Professional organizations often have job listings available to members. They also publish journals and newsletters to keep members up-to-date on new developments in the field.

If you are looking to be a self-employed conservator, you may wish to volunteer your services until you have established yourself. Volunteering to assist nonprofit organizations with their conservation needs will give you good exposure and help you learn more about book conservation and the skills that potential clients are seeking.

ADVANCEMENT

Book conservators who demonstrate a high level of skill in their craft can move on to positions with more responsibility. They may be called upon to train assistants in book conservation or to teach conservation techniques at a college, certification program, or conservation lab.

They may also transfer their skill in dealing with rare and fine materials and work more in the art community as art conservators, appraisers, or artists. With more experience and education, a book conservator can become an archivist, curator, or librarian. Many book conservators prefer to move away from full-time conservation and work on freelance projects instead.

With advanced computer knowledge, book conservators can help bring rare and fragile materials into the digital age. They may learn how to make materials available on the Internet and become virtual curators. They may also move on to actual exhibition work. Knowing how to preserve materials gives them the advantage in exhibiting them safely.

As book conservators gain more prominent positions, the trend is away from materials and toward administration. Beginning conservators will often spend most of their day dealing directly with the materials to be conserved. Conservators who move on to more advanced positions generally spend more time training others; evaluating materials and methods; dealing with outside suppliers, customers, and associations; attending meetings; and planning for the future of the department and the field.

EARNINGS

It is difficult to say how much the average book conservator earns, since many conservators work part time, are self-employed, or have positions that encompass other duties as well. In general, the salary range for book conservators may fall within the range the U.S. Department of Labor reports for all conservators. In 2006, this group of professionals had a median annual income of $34,340. The lowest paid 10 percent earned less than $20,600 yearly, and the highest paid 10 percent made more than $61,270 per year. Often the size of the employer affects how much a conservator earns, with larger employers able to pay more. In addition, book conservators in major metropolitan areas generally earn more than those in small cities, and those with greater skills also command higher salaries.

Conservators who work for libraries, conservation organizations, large corporations, institutions, or government agencies generally receive a full range of benefits, including health care coverage, vacation days, paid holidays, paid sick time, and retirement savings plans. Self-employed book conservators usually have to provide their own benefits. All conservators have the added benefit of working with rare and unique materials. They have the opportunity to work with history and preserve an artifact for the future.

WORK ENVIRONMENT

Because of the damage that dirt, humidity, and the sun can cause to books, most conservators work in clean, climate-controlled areas away from direct sunlight. Many conservation labs are small offices, which often employ the conservator alone or perhaps with one or two part-time assistants. Other labs are part of a larger department within an organization; the University of Chicago's Regenstein Library, for instance, has a conservation lab within the Special Collections department. With this type of arrangement, the book conservator generally has a few student and nonstudent assistants who work part time to help with some of the conservation duties.

Book conservators are always on the move. They use their hands constantly to measure, cut, and paste materials. They also bend, lift, and twist in order to reach items they work on and make room for new materials. Also, books are not always an easy size or weight to handle. Some oversized items need to be transported on a book truck from the stack area to the conservation area for treatment.

Most book conservators work 40 hours a week, usually during regular, weekday working hours. Depending on the needs of their department and the clientele they serve, book conservators may need to be available some weekend hours. Also, some book conservators may agree to travel to the homes of clients to view materials that may require conservation.

OUTLOOK

Employment for book conservators will grow about as fast as the average for all occupations through 2014. The U.S. Department of Labor notes that while the outlook for conservators in general is favorable, there is strong competition for jobs. Book conservators who are graduates of conservation programs and are willing to relocate should have the best opportunities for employment. Those who can use their conservation skills in tandem with other abilities may also find more job openings. Book conservators with an artistic bent, for instance, could bring their conservation skills to an exhibition program at an art museum. Conservators who enjoy public contact could use their practical experience to teach classes in conservation techniques.

Some people are concerned that our increasingly digital society will create fewer opportunities for book conservators. They claim that new technologies, such as television, computers, telephones, and the Internet have changed communication styles so drastically that printed books will eventually become obsolete. While it is true that more advanced technology will bring new challenges to conservation, these advances should also increase opportunities for conservators who can blend these developments with traditional conservation efforts. For example, a book conservator with excellent computer skills and Web-authoring knowledge can work on a project to digitize rare book collections and make them available to people all over the world.

FOR MORE INFORMATION

For certification information, contact
Academy of Certified Archivists
90 State Street, Suite 1009
Albany, NY 12207-1716
Tel: 518-463-8644
Email: aca@caphill.com
http://www.certifiedarchivists.org

For information about how to become a conservator, contact
American Institute for Conservation of Historic and Artistic Works
1156 15th Street, NW, Suite 320
Washington, DC 20005-1714
Tel: 202-452-9545
Email: info@aic-faic.org
http://aic.stanford.edu

For information on book conservation, contact
Guild of Book Workers
521 Fifth Avenue
New York, NY 10175-0038
http://palimpsest.stanford.edu/byorg/gbw

For information about preservation methods, services, and opportunities, contact
Library of Congress Preservation Directorate
101 Independence Avenue, SE
Washington, DC 20540-4500
Tel: 202-707-5213
http://lcweb.loc.gov/preserv

For a wealth of information about conservation topics, check out this project of the Preservation Department of Stanford University Libraries and Academic Information Resources
Conservation OnLine
http://palimpsest.stanford.edu

College Professors, Art

QUICK FACTS

School Subjects
Art
Art history
Speech

Personal Skills
Communication/ideas
Helping/teaching

Work Environment
Primarily indoors
Primarily one location

Minimum Education Level
Master's degree

Salary Range
$29,290 to $53,160 to
$94,270+

Certification or Licensing
None available

Outlook
Much faster than the average

DOT
090

GOE
12.03.02

NOC
4121

O*NET-SOC
25-1121.00

OVERVIEW

College and university faculty members teach art at junior colleges or at four-year colleges and universities. Most art professors teach in a specific and highly specialized art form, such as sculpture or painting. They also teach classes in non-studio art, such as art therapy, art criticism and history, art education, and art administration.

In addition to teaching, most art faculty members continue to produce art, conduct research and write publications. Art professors may show their work in galleries or publish their research findings in various scholarly journals. The more a professor shows or publishes work, the more likely the professor can advance to becoming permanent, tenured faculty. There are approximately 78,000 art, drama, and music postsecondary teachers employed in the United States.

HISTORY

Until the mid-1500s, most early artists in the West learned their craft via one-on-one instruction with masters. Others learned commercial art through membership in craft guilds, associations of craftworkers in a particular occupational field. Guilds were gradually replaced by art academies. The Accademia del Disegno in Florence, Italy—founded in 1562—was one of the first such academies, according to A History of Art Education, a Web site developed by art education graduate students at the University of North Texas. Its founders had a goal of passing on the knowledge of the old masters, while helping students to become successful in their own right. In 1648, the French Academy of Painting and Sculpture was established to train aspiring artists. The curriculum was demanding, and was based on the classical style. Students learned the mathematical principles of art and participated in life drawing classes in which live models were sketched.

In the United States, art education was largely informal until the 1800s when art academies began to be founded. The Pennsylvania Academy of the Fine Arts was founded in 1805 by Charles Willson Peale, William Rush, and other artists. It was the first art museum and art school in the United States. Students learned artistic techniques by copying the works of masters, but eventually began learning via life drawing classes. The school is still open today.

In 1873, the Massachusetts Normal Art School (known today as the Massachusetts College of Art) was founded. It was one of the first schools to prepare drawing teachers. By 1879, 201 students had earned certificates—with slightly more than half employed as drawing instructors.

In the following decades, many other colleges and universities added art programs in painting, sculpture, art history, art conservation, art therapy, and other artistic fields.

The National Art Education Association was formed in 1947 to represent the professional interests of art educators. It had 3,500 members at its formation. Today, it has approximately 22,000 members.

THE JOB

College and university faculty members teach art and related subjects at junior colleges or at four-year colleges and universities. At four-year institutions, most faculty members are *instructors, assistant professors, associate professors,* or *full professors.* These four types of academic rank differ in regards to status, job responsibilities, and salary. Instructors and assistant professors are new faculty members who are working to get tenure (status as a permanent professor); they seek to advance to associate and then to full professorships.

The most important responsibility of college art professors is to teach students. Their role within a college art department will determine the level of courses they teach and the number of courses per semester. Most professors work with students at all levels, from college freshmen to graduate students. They may head several classes a semester or only a few each year. Some of their classes will have large enrollment, while graduate seminars may consist of only 12 or fewer students. Though college professors may spend fewer than 10 hours a week in the actual classroom, they spend many hours preparing lectures and lesson plans, grading artwork, papers, and exams, and preparing grade reports. They also schedule office hours during the week to be available to students outside of the art studio or lecture hall, and they meet with students individually throughout the semester. In some courses—such as those that focus on art conservation and restoration—they rely heavily on laboratories to transmit course material. Many professors teaching this discipline also work in the field as practicing artists, art historians, art conservators, and in other art-related professions.

In the classroom/studio, art professors teach classes on such topics as beginning painting, advanced painting, photographic image making, beginning drawing, ceramics, fiber/material studies, computer animation, Web art, basic metalsmithing, modern and postmodern art, curatorial practice, and museum education.

Another important responsibility is advising students. Not all art professors serve as advisers, but those who do must set aside large blocks of time to guide students through the program. College art professors who serve as advisers may have any number of students assigned to them, from fewer than 10 to more than 100, depending on the administrative policies of the college. Their responsibility may involve looking over a planned program of studies to make sure the students meet requirements for graduation, or it may involve working intensively with each student on many aspects of college life.

The third responsibility of art professors is research and publication. Faculty members who are heavily involved in research programs sometimes are assigned a smaller teaching load. College professors publish their research findings in various scholarly journals such as *the Art Bulletin* and *Art Journal*. They also write books based on their research or on their own knowledge and experience in the field. Most textbooks are written by college and university teachers. Art professors also practice their craft and exhibit their artwork in various ways. For example, a painter or photographer will have gallery showings.

Some faculty members eventually rise to the position of *art department chair,* where they govern the affairs of their entire department. Department chairs, faculty, and other professional staff members are aided in their myriad duties by *graduate assistants,* who may help develop teaching materials, conduct research, give examinations, teach lower-level courses, and carry out other activities.

Some college art professors may also conduct classes in an extension program. In such a program, they teach evening and weekend courses for the benefit of people who otherwise would not be able to take advantage of the institution's resources. They may travel away from the campus and meet with a group of students at another location. They may work full time for the extension division or may divide their time between on-campus and off-campus teaching.

The *junior college art instructor* has many of the same respon-sibilities as teachers in a four-year college or university. Because junior colleges offer only a two-year program, they teach only undergraduates.

REQUIREMENTS

High School
Take as many art classes as possible in high school to learn about the variety of career options in the field. Your high school's college preparatory program likely includes courses in English, science, foreign language, history, math, and government. In addition, you should take courses in speech to get a sense of what it will be like to lecture to a group of students. Your school's debate team can also help you develop public speaking skills, along with research skills.

Postsecondary Training
For prospective professors, you will need at least one advanced degree in art. The master's degree is considered the minimum stan-dard, and graduate work beyond the master's is usually desirable. If you hope to advance in academic rank above instructor, most institutions require a doctorate. Your graduate school program will be similar to a life of teaching—in addition to attending seminars, you'll do research, prepare articles for publication, and teach some undergraduate courses.

You may find employment in a junior college with only a master's degree. Advancement in responsibility and in salary, however, is more likely to come if you have earned a doctorate.

Other Requirements
To be successful in this career, you should enjoy creating and teach-ing art. People skills are important because you'll be dealing directly with students, administrators, and other faculty members on a daily basis. You should feel comfortable in a role of authority and possess self-confidence. You should always be willing to learn new artistic techniques and teaching methods.

EXPLORING

Your high school art teachers use many of the same skills as college professors, so talk to your teachers about their careers and their college experiences. You can develop your own teaching experi-ence by volunteering at a community center, working at a day care center, or working at a summer camp (especially one that focuses on art). Also, spend some time on a college campus to get a sense of the environment. Write to colleges for their admissions brochures and course catalogs (or check them out online); read about the faculty members in art departments and the courses they teach. Before visiting college campuses, make arrangements to speak to professors who teach courses that interest you. These professors may allow you to sit in on their classes and observe. Also, make appointments with college advisers and with people in the admissions and recruitment offices. If your grades are good enough, you might be able to serve as a teaching assistant during your undergraduate years, which can give you experience leading discussions and grading papers.

EMPLOYERS

Art professors teach in undergraduate and graduate programs. The teaching jobs at doctoral institutions are usually better paying and more prestigious. The most sought-after positions are those that offer tenure. Teachers who have only a master's degree will be limited to opportunities with junior colleges, community colleges, and some small private institutions. There are approximately 78,000 art, drama, and music postsecondary teachers employed in the United States.

STARTING OUT

You should start the process of finding a teaching position while you are in graduate school. The process includes developing a curriculum vitae (a detailed, academic resume), preparing slides or other samples of your scholarly creative work, writing an artist statement (when applicable), writing for publication, assisting with research, attending conferences, and gaining teaching experience and recommendations. Many students begin applying for teaching positions while finishing their graduate program. For most positions at four-year institutions, you must travel to large conferences where interviews can be arranged with representatives from the universities to which you have applied.

Because of the competition for tenure-track positions, you may have to work for a few years in temporary positions, visiting various schools as an adjunct professor. Some professional associations maintain lists of teaching opportunities in their areas. They may also make lists of applicants available to college administrators looking to fill an available position.

ADVANCEMENT

At the college level, the normal pattern of advancement is from art instructor to assistant professor, to associate professor, to full professor. All four academic ranks are concerned primarily with teaching and research. College faculty members who have an interest in and a talent for administration may be advanced to chair of the art department. A few become college or university presidents or other types of administrators.

The instructor is usually an inexperienced college teacher. He or she may hold a doctorate or may have completed all the Ph.D. requirements except for the dissertation. Most colleges look upon the rank of instructor as the period during which the college is trying out the teacher. Instructors usually are advanced to the position of assistant professor within three to four years. Assistant professors are given up to about six years to prove themselves worthy of tenure, and if they do so, they become associate professors. Some professors choose to remain at the associate level. Others strive to become full professors and receive greater status, salary, and responsibilities.

Most colleges have clearly defined promotion policies from rank to rank for faculty members, and many have written statements about the number of years in which instructors and assistant professors may remain in grade. Administrators in many colleges hope to encourage younger faculty members to increase their skills and competencies and thus to qualify for the more responsible positions of associate professor and full professor.

EARNINGS

College art professors' earnings vary depending on the size of the school, the type of school (public, private, women's only, etc.), and by the level of position the professor holds. The U.S. Department of Labor reports that the median annual salary for postsecondary art teachers was $53,160 in 2006. Of college art teachers, 10 percent earned $29,290 or less and 10 percent earned $94,270 or more.

Benefits for art teachers typically include health insurance, sick pay, 401(k) plans, and reimbursement for continuing education. Full-time college faculty may also receive stipends for travel related to research, housing allowances, and tuition waivers for dependents.

WORK ENVIRONMENT

A college or university is usually a pleasant place in which to work. Campuses bustle with all types of activities and events, stimulating

Summer Art Programs

If you're interested in a career in art, participating in a summer program offered by a college or university is a great way to learn more about the field. In these programs, you'll get the chance to be taught by well-known artists, learn new artistic techniques, and interact with students just like you who are interested in art. Most importantly, you'll get a chance to try out a career in art before college. The following is a short list of summer art programs for high school students:

Boston University (Boston, Mass.)
High School Honors Program/Summer Challenge Program
Tel: 617-353-1378
Email: buhssumr@bu.edu
http://www.bu.edu/summer/highschool

Columbia College Chicago (Chicago, Ill.)
High School Summer Institute
Tel: 312-344-7130
Email: summerinstitute@colum.edu
http://www.colum.edu/admissions/hssi.php

Cornell University (Ithaca, N.Y.)
Summer College
Tel: 607-255-6203
http://www.sce.cornell.edu/sc/explorations/art.php

University of Denver (Denver, Colo.)
Early Experience Program
Tel: 303-871-3452
Email: city@du.edu
http://www.du.edu/city/programs/year-round-programs/early-experience-program.html

University of Maryland (College Park, Md.)
The Arts! At Maryland
Tel: 301-314-8240
http://www.summer.umd.edu/c/admissions/courses/taam

Michigan Technological University (Houghton, Mich.)
Summer Youth Program
Tel: 906-487-2219
http://youthprograms.mtu.edu

Rochester Institute of Technology (Rochester, N.Y.)
College and Careers Program
Tel: 585-475-6631
http://ambassador.rit.edu/careers2007

Southern Methodist University (Dallas, Tex.)
Talented and Gifted Program/College Experience Program/
Summer Youth Program
Tel: 214-768-2000
http://www.smu.edu/continuing_education/youth

University of South Carolina (Columbia, S.C.)
Youth Academic Programs
Tel: 803-777-9444
http://ced.sc.edu/adventures

Stanford University (Stanford, Calif.)
Summer College for High School Students
Tel: 650-723-3109
Email: summersession@stanford.edu
http://summer.stanford.edu

Syracuse University (Syracuse, N.Y.)
High School Summer College
Tel: 315-443-5297
Email: sumcoll@syr.edu
http://summercollege.syr.edu

Washington University in St. Louis (St. Louis, Mo.)
Portfolio Plus
Tel: 314-935-6532
Email: artinfo@wustl.edu
http://www.arch.wustl.edu/art/otherPrograms/summer_
programs.html

University of Wisconsin–Green Bay (Green Bay, Wisc.)
Summer Art Studio
Tel: 800-892-2118
Email: summercamps@uwgb.edu
http://www.uwgb.edu/camps

ideas, and a young, energetic population. Much prestige comes with success as a professor, artist, and scholar; art professors have the respect of students, colleagues, and others in their community.

Depending on the size of the department, college art professors may have their own office, or they may have to share an office and studio with one or more colleagues. Their department may provide them with a computer, Internet access, and research assistants. College professors can arrange their schedule around class hours, academic meetings, and the established office hours when they meet with students. Most college art teachers work more than 40 hours each week. Although college professors may teach only two or three classes a semester, they spend many hours preparing for classes, examining student work, and conducting research.

OUTLOOK

The U.S. Department of Labor predicts much faster than average employment growth for college and university professors through 2014. College enrollment is projected to grow due to an increased number of 18- to 24-year-olds, an increased number of adults returning to college, and an increased number of foreign-born students. Retirement of current faculty members will also provide job openings. However, competition for full-time, tenure-track positions at four-year schools will be very strong. Prospective art professors who are qualified, talented, and flexible (willing to move—even to another state) will have the best employment opportunities.

FOR MORE INFORMATION

To read about the issues affecting college professors, contact the following organizations:

American Association of University Professors
1012 14th Street, NW, Suite 500
Washington, DC 20005-3465
Tel: 202-737-5900
Email: aaup@aaup.org
http://www.aaup.org

American Federation of Teachers
555 New Jersey Avenue, NW
Washington, DC 20001-2029
Tel: 202-879-4400
http://www.aft.org

The CAA is a professional organization for art teachers and researchers.

College Art Association (CAA)
275 Seventh Avenue, 18th Floor
New York, NY 10001-6708
Tel: 212-691-1051
Email: nyoffice@collegeart.org
http://www.collegeart.org

For information on student membership and useful publications, contact

National Art Education Association
1916 Association Drive
Reston, VA 20191-1590
Tel: 703-860-8000
Email: info@naea-reston.org
http://www.naea-reston.org

For information on accredited teacher education programs and teaching careers, contact

National Council for Accreditation of Teacher Education
2010 Massachusetts Avenue, NW, Suite 500
Washington, DC 20036-1023
Tel: 202-466-7496
http://www.ncate.org

Contact the council for information on student membership, conferences, fellowships, and a list of U.S. programs offering degrees in ceramics.

National Council on Education for the Ceramic Arts
77 Erie Village Square, Suite 280
Erie, CO 80516-6996
Tel: 866-266-2322
Email: office@nceca.net
http://www.nceca.net

Conservators and Conservation Technicians

QUICK FACTS

School Subjects
Art
Chemistry

Personal Skills
Mechanical/manipulative
Technical/scientific

Work Environment
Primarily indoors
Primarily one location

Minimum Education Level
Bachelor's degree

Salary Range
$20,600 to $34,340 to
$61,270+

Certification or Licensing
None available

Outlook
About as fast as the average

DOT
102

GOE
12.03.04

NOC
5112, 5212

O*NET-SOC
25-4013.00

OVERVIEW

Conservators analyze and assess the condition of artifacts and pieces of art, plan for the care of art collections, and carry out conservation treatments and programs. Conservators may be in private practice or work for museums, historical societies, or state institutions. When conserving artifacts or artwork, these professionals must select methods and materials that preserve and retain the original integrity of each piece. Conservators must be knowledgeable about the objects in their care, which may be natural objects, such as bones and fossils, or man-made objects, such as paintings, sculpture, paper, and metal.

Conservation technicians work under the supervision of conservators and complete maintenance work on the collection.

HISTORY

Conservation is the youngest of all museum disciplines. The word *conservation* has been used in reference to works of art only since approximately 1930. For at least a century before 1930, museums may have employed restorers, or restoration specialists, but the philosophy that guided their work was much different than the ideas and values held by conservators today. Early conservators were often craftspeople, artists, or framers called upon to restore a damaged work of art to an approximate version of its original condition. They repainted, varnished, or patched objects as they saw fit, working independently and experimenting as necessary to achieve the desired results. Conservators today use highly scientific methods and recognize the need both to care for works of art before deterioration occurs and to treat objects after damage has been done. A key guiding principle in conservation is to avoid introducing changes in a work that are irreversible.

The first regional conservation laboratory in the United States, known as the Intermuseum Conservation Association, was created in 1952, in Oberlin, Ohio, when several smaller museums joined to bring their skills together.

Thanks to increasingly precise cleaning methods and scientific inventions such as thermal adhesives, the science of conservation has advanced. Today, the field is highly specialized and those who work in it must face demanding standards and challenges.

THE JOB

Conservation professionals generally choose to specialize in one area of work defined by a medium, such as in the preservation of books and paper, architecture, objects, photographic materials, paintings, textiles, or wooden artifacts. There are also conservators who specialize in archaeology or ethnographic materials. Many are employed by museums, while others provide services through private practice. Conservation activities include carrying out technical and scientific studies on art objects, stabilizing the structure and reintegrating the appearance of cultural artifacts, and establishing the environment in which artifacts are best preserved. A conservator's responsibilities also may include documenting the structure and condition through written and visual recording, designing programs for preventive care, and executing conservation treatments. Conservation tools include microscopes and cameras and equipment for specialized processes such as infrared and ultraviolet photography and X rays.

Conservation technicians assist conservators in preserving or restoring artifacts and art objects. To do this, they study descriptions and information about the object, and may perform chemical and physical tests as specified by the conservator. If an object is metal, a technician may be instructed to clean it by scraping or by applying chemical solvents. Statues are washed with soap solutions, and furniture and silver are polished.

When a repair is necessary, conservation technicians may be asked to reassemble the broken pieces using glue or solder (a metallic substance used to join metal surfaces), then buff the object when the repair is complete. They may repaint objects where the original paint is faded or missing, making sure to use paint of the same chemical composition and color as the original. Technicians may also make and repair picture frames and mount paintings in frames.

A *conservation scientist* is a professional scientist whose primary focus is in developing materials and knowledge to support conservation activities. Some specialize in scientific research into artists' materials, such as paints and varnishes. *Conservation educators* have substantial knowledge and experience in the theory and practice of conservation, and have chosen to direct their efforts toward teaching the principles, methodology, and technical aspects of the profession. *Preparators* supervise the installation of specimens, art objects, and artifacts, often working with design technicians, curators, and directors to ensure the safety and preservation of items on display.

REQUIREMENTS

High School

Good conservation work comes from a well-balanced formulation of art and science. To prepare for a career in conservation, concentrate on doing well in all academic subjects, including courses in chemistry, natural science, history, and the arts.

Postsecondary Training

In the past, many conservation professionals earned their training solely through apprenticeships with esteemed conservators. The same is not true today; you will need a bachelor's degree to find work as a technician, and in all but the smallest institutions you will need a master's degree to advance to conservator. Because graduate programs are highly selective, you should plan your academic path with care.

At the undergraduate level, take coursework in the sciences, including inorganic and organic chemistry, the humanities (art history, archaeology, and anthropology), and studio art. If you do not go to a university that has an undergraduate program in art conservation, you should consult the graduate programs in art conservation about the courses necessary to take in college so that you are properly prepared.

Some graduate programs will consider work experience and gained expertise in conservation practice as comparable to coursework when screening applicants. In addition, most graduate programs recognize a student's participation in apprenticeship or internship positions while also completing coursework as indicative of the applicant's commitment to the career. Graduate programs typically last three or four years, with the final year being an internship year. This final year involves working full time in a chosen conservation specialty under the guidance of an experienced conservator. The American Institute for Conservation of Historic and Artistic Works offers links to educational programs at its Web site, http://aic.stanford.edu/education/becoming.

Other Requirements

Conservation can be physically demanding. Conservators and conservation technicians need to be able to concentrate on specific physical and mental tasks for long periods of time. Endurance, manual dexterity, and patience are often needed to complete projects successfully.

Work on one piece of art could take months or even years; because of the fragile nature of the materials, conservation work should never be rushed.

Finally, an important personal quality to have for this line of work is a respect and love for art. Conservators should appreciate the value in all art forms (regardless of personal bias) and treat all pieces that they work on with the utmost care.

EXPLORING

If you are considering a career in the conservation of art or artifacts, try contacting local museums or art conservation laboratories that may allow tours or interviews. Read trade or technical journals to gain a sense of the many issues addressed by conservators. Contact professional organizations, such as the American Institute for Conservation of Historic and Artistic Works, for directories of training and conservation programs.

Because employment in this field, even at entry level, most often entails the handling of precious materials and cultural resources, you should be fairly well prepared before contacting professionals to request either internship or volunteer positions. You need to demonstrate a high level of academic achievement and have a serious interest in the career to edge out the competition for a limited number of jobs.

EMPLOYERS

Museums, libraries, historical societies, private conservation laboratories, and government agencies hire conservators and conservation technicians. Institutions with small operating budgets sometimes

Mean Earnings by Industry, 2006

Federal government	$43,880
Colleges, universities, and professional schools	$38,200
State government	$37,820
Museums, historical sites, and similar institutions	$34,640
Local government	$32,650

Source: U.S. Department of Labor

hire part-time specialists to perform conservation work. This is especially common when curators need extra help in preparing items for display. Antique dealers may also seek the expertise of an experienced conservator for merchandise restoration, identification, and appraisal purposes.

STARTING OUT

Most often, students entering the field of art conservation have completed high school and undergraduate studies, and many are contemplating graduate programs. At this point a student is ready to seek a position (often unpaid) as an apprentice or intern with either a private conservation company or a museum to gain a practical feel for the work. Training opportunities are scarce and in high demand. Prospective students must convince potential trainers of their dedication to the highly demanding craft of conservation. The combination of academic or formal training along with hands-on experience and apprenticeship is the ideal foundation for entering the career.

ADVANCEMENT

Due to rapid changes in each conservation specialty, practicing conservators must keep abreast with advances in technology and methodology. Conservators stay up-to-date by reading publications, attending professional meetings, and enrolling in short-term workshops or courses.

An experienced conservator wishing to move into another realm of the field may become a private consultant, an appraiser of art or artifacts, a conservation educator, a curator, or a museum registrar.

EARNINGS

Salaries for conservators vary greatly depending on the level of experience, chosen specialty, region, job description, and employer. Conservators and museum technicians had median annual earnings of $34,340 in 2006, according to the U.S. Department of Labor. The lowest paid 10 percent of this group earned less than $20,600, and the highest paid 10 percent made more than $61,270.

According to the American Institute for Conservation of Historic and Artistic Works, a first-year conservator can expect to earn approximately $20,000 annually. Conservators with several years of experience report annual earnings between $35,000 and $40,000. Senior conservators have reported earnings between $50,000 and $60,000 annually.

Fringe benefits, including paid vacations, medical and dental insurance, sick leave, and retirement plans, vary according to each employer's policies.

WORK ENVIRONMENT

Conservation work may be conducted indoors, in laboratories, or in an outdoor setting. Conservators typically work 40–60 hours per week, depending on exhibition schedules and deadlines, as well as the number and condition of unstable objects in their collections. Because some conservation tasks and techniques involve the use of toxic chemicals, laboratories are equipped with ventilation systems. At times a conservator may find it necessary to wear a mask and possibly even a respirator when working with particularly harsh chemicals or varnishes. Most of the work requires meticulous attention to detail, a great deal of precision, and manual dexterity.

The rewards of the conservation profession are the satisfaction of preserving artifacts that reflect the diversity of human achievements; being in regular contact with art, artifacts, and structures; enjoying a stimulating workplace; and the creative application of expertise to the preservation of artistically and historically significant objects.

OUTLOOK

Employment of archivists, curators, and museum technicians (which includes conservators and technicians) will grow at an average rate through 2014, according to the U.S. Department of Labor. Competition for these desirable positions, however, will be strong.

The public's developing interest in cultural material of all forms will contribute to art conservation and preservation as a growing field. New specialties have emerged in response to the interest in collections maintenance and preventive care. Conservation, curatorial, and registration responsibilities are intermingling and creating hybrid conservation professional titles, such as collections care, environmental monitoring, and exhibits specialists.

Despite these developments, however, any decreases in federal funding often affect employment and educational opportunities. For example, in any given year, if Congress limits government assistance to the National Endowment for the Arts, fewer funds are available to arts-related organizations and for grants to artists. As museums experience a tightening of federal or state funds, many may choose to decrease the number of paid conservators on staff and instead may rely on a small staff augmented by private conservation companies that can be contracted on a short-term basis as necessary. Private industry and for-profit companies may then continue to grow, while federally funded nonprofit museums may experience a reduction of staff.

FOR MORE INFORMATION

To receive additional information on conservation training, contact
American Institute for Conservation of Historic and Artistic Works
1156 15th Street, NW, Suite 320
Washington, DC 20005-1714
Tel: 202-452-9545
Email: info@aic-faic.org
http://aic.stanford.edu

For information on internships and other learning opportunities in Canada, contact
Canadian Conservation Institute
1030 Innes Road
Ottawa, ON K1A 0M5
Canada
Tel: 613-998-3721
http://www.cci-icc.gc.ca

Costume Designers

OVERVIEW

Costume designers plan, create, and maintain clothing and accessories for all characters in a stage, film, television, dance, or opera production. Designers custom fit each character, and either create a new garment or alter an existing costume.

HISTORY

Costume design has been an important part of the theater since the early Greek tragedies, when actors generally wore masks and long robes with sleeves. By the time of the Roman Caesars, stage costumes had become very elaborate and colorful.

After the fall of Rome, theater disappeared for some time, but later returned in the form of Easter and Nativity plays. Priests and choirboys wore their usual robes with some simple additions, such as veils and crowns. Plays then moved from the church to the marketplace, and costumes again became important to the production.

During the Renaissance, costumes were designed for the Italian pageants, the French ballets, and the English masques by such famous designers as Torelli, Jean Berain, and Burnacini. From 1760 to 1782, Louis-Rene Boquet designed costumes using wide panniers, forming a kind of elaborate ballet skirt. But by the end of the 18th century, there was a movement toward more classical costumes on the stage.

During the early 19th century, historical costumes became popular, and period details were added to contemporary dress. Toward the end of the 19th century, realism became important, and actors wore the dress of the day, often their own clothes. Because this trend resulted in less work for the costume designers, they turned to musical and opera productions to express their creativity.

In the early 20th century, Diaghilev's Russian Ballet introduced a non-naturalistic style in costumes, most notably in the designs of Leon Bakst. This trend gave way to European avant-garde theater, in which costumes became abstract and symbolic.

Since the 1960s, new materials, such as plastics and adhesives, have greatly increased the costume designer's range. Today, their work is prominent in plays, musicals, dance performances, films, music videos, and television programs.

THE JOB

Costume designers generally work as freelancers. After they have been contracted to provide the costumes for a production, they read the script to learn about the theme, location, time period, character types, dialogue, and action. They meet with the director to discuss his or her feelings on the plot, characters, period and style, time frame for the production, and budget.

For a play, designers plan a rough costume plot, which is a list of costume changes by scene for each character. They thoroughly research the history and setting in which the play is set. They plan a preliminary color scheme and sketch the costumes, including details such as gloves, footwear, hose, purses, jewelry, canes, fans, bouquets, and other props. The costume designer or an assistant collects swatches of fabrics and samples of various accessories.

After completing the research, final color sketches are painted or drawn and mounted for presentation. Once the director approves the designs, the costume designer solicits bids from contractors, creates or rents costumes, and shops for fabrics and accessories. Measurements of all actors are taken. Designers work closely with drapers, sewers, hairstylists, and makeup artists in the costume shop. They supervise fittings and attend all dress rehearsals to make final adjustments and repairs.

Costume designers also work in films, television, and videos, aiming to provide the look that will highlight characters' personalities. Aside from working with actors, they may also design and create costumes for performers such as figure skaters, ballroom dance competitors, circus members, theme park characters, rock artists, and others who routinely wear costumes as part of a show.

REQUIREMENTS

High School
Costume designers need at least a high school education. It is helpful to take classes in art, home economics, and theater and to participate

in drama clubs or community theater. English, literature, and history classes will help you learn how to analyze a play and research the clothing and manner of various historical periods. Marketing and business-related classes will also be helpful, as most costume designers work as freelancers. Familiarity with computers is useful, as many designers work with computer-aided design (CAD) programs.

While in high school, consider starting a portfolio of design sketches. Practicing in a sketchbook is a great way to get ideas and designs out on paper and organized for future reference. You can also get design ideas through others; watch theater, television, or movie productions and take note of the characters' dress. Sketch them on your own for practice. Looking through fashion magazines can also give you ideas to sketch.

Postsecondary Training

A college degree is not a requirement, but in this highly competitive field, it gives a sizable advantage. Most costume designers today have a bachelor's degree. Many art schools, especially in New York and Los Angeles, have programs in costume design at both the bachelor's and master's degree level. A liberal arts school with a strong theater program is also a good choice.

Other Requirements

Costume designers need sewing, draping, and patterning skills, as well as training in basic design techniques and figure drawing. Aside from being artistic, designers must also be able to work with people because many compromises and agreements must be made between the designer and the production's director.

Costume designers must prepare a portfolio of their work, including photographs and sketches highlighting their best efforts. Some theatrical organizations require membership in United Scenic Artists (USA), a union that protects the interests of designers on the job and sets minimum fees. Students in design programs who pass an exam and have some design experience can apply for USA's Designer Apprentice Program. More experienced designers who want full professional membership in the union must also submit a portfolio for review.

EXPLORING

If you are interested in costume design, consider joining a theater organization, such as a school drama club or a community theater. School dance troupes or film classes also may offer opportunities to explore costume design.

The Costume Designer's Handbook: A Complete Guide for Amateur and Professional Costume Designers, by Rosemary Ingham and

Liz Covey (Portsmouth, N.H.: Heinemann, 1992), is an invaluable resource for beginning or experienced costume designers.

You can practice designing on your own, by drawing original sketches or copying designs from television, films, or the stage. Practice sewing and altering costumes from sketches for yourself, friends and family.

EMPLOYERS

Costume designers are employed by production companies that produce works for stage, television, and film. Most employers are located in New York and Los Angeles, although most metropolitan areas have community theater and film production companies that hire designers.

STARTING OUT

Most high schools and colleges have drama clubs and dance groups that need costumes designed and made. Community theaters, too, may offer opportunities to assist in costume production. Regional theaters hire several hundred costume technicians each year for seasons that vary from 28 to 50 weeks.

Many beginning designers enter the field by becoming an assistant to a designer. Many established designers welcome newcomers and can be generous mentors. Some beginning workers start out in costume shops, which usually require membership in a union. However, non-union workers may be allowed to work for short-term projects. Some designers begin as *shoppers,* who obtain swatches of fabrics, compare prices, and buy yardage, trim, and accessories. Shoppers learn where to find the best materials at reasonable prices and often establish valuable contacts in the field. Other starting positions include *milliner's assistant, craft assistant,* or *assistant to the draper.*

Schools with bachelor's and master's programs in costume design may offer internships that can lead to jobs after graduation. Another method of entering costume design is to contact regional theaters directly and send your resume to the theater's managing director.

Before you become a costume designer, you may want to work as a freelance design assistant for a few years to gain helpful experience, a reputation, contacts, and an impressive portfolio.

ADVANCEMENT

Beginning designers must show they are willing to do a variety of tasks. The theater community is small and intricately interconnected, so those who work hard and are flexible with assignments can gain good reputations quickly. Smaller regional theaters tend to hire designers for a full season to work with the same people on one or more productions, so opportunities for movement may be scarce. Eventually, costume designers with experience and talent can work for larger productions, such as films, television, and videos.

EARNINGS

Earnings vary greatly in this business depending on factors such as how many outfits the designer completes, how long they are employed during the year, and the amount of their experience. Although the U.S. Department of Labor does not provide salary figures for costume designers, it does report that the related occupational group of tailors, dressmakers, and custom sewers had a median hourly wage of $11.01 in 2006. For full-time work, this hourly wage translates into a yearly income of approximately $22,910. However, those just starting out and working as assistants earned as little as $7.32 an hour, translating into an annual salary of approximately $15,230. The most experienced tailors, dressmakers, and custom sewers earned $17.63 an hour (or $36,680) or more annually.

Costume designers who work on Broadway or for other large stage productions are usually members of the United Scenic Artists union, which sets minimum fees, requires producers to pay into pension and welfare funds, protects the designer's rights, establishes rules for billing, and offers group health and life insurance.

According to the union, a costume designer for a Broadway show in 2006 earned anywhere from $6,758 (for creating costumes for shows with one to seven characters) to $32,181 (for shows with 36 or more characters). For opera and dance companies, salary is usually by costume count. Costume designers working on major film or television productions earned union minimums of $2,515 for five days of work in 2006.

For feature films and television, costume designers earn daily rates for an eight-hour day or a weekly rate for an unlimited number of hours. Designers sometimes earn royalties on their designs.

Regional theaters usually set individual standard fees, which vary widely, beginning around $200 per week for an assistant. Most of them do not require membership in the union.

Most costume designers work freelance and are paid per costume or show. Costume designers can charge $90–$500 per costume, but some costumes, such as those for figure skaters, can cost thousands of dollars. Freelance costume designers often receive a flat rate for designing costumes for a show. For small and regional theaters, this rate may be in the $400–$500 range; the flat rate for medium and large productions generally starts at around $1,000. Many costume designers must take second part-time or full-time jobs to supplement their income from costume design.

Freelancers are responsible for their own health insurance, life insurance, and pension plans. They do not receive holiday, sick, or vacation pay.

WORK ENVIRONMENT

Costume designers put in long hours at painstaking detail work. It is a demanding profession that requires flexible, artistic, and practical workers. The schedule can be erratic—a busy period followed by weeks of little or no work. Though costumes are often a crucial part of a production's success, designers usually get little recognition compared to the actors and director.

Designers meet a variety of interesting and gifted people. Every play, film, or concert is different and every production situation is unique, so there is rarely a steady routine. Costume designers must play many roles: artist, sewer, researcher, buyer, manager, and negotiator.

OUTLOOK

The U.S. Department of Labor predicts that employment for tailors, dressmakers, and skilled sewers will grow more slowly than the average of all occupations through 2014, and costume designers may not fair much better. The health of the entertainment business, especially theater, is very dependent on the overall economy and public attitudes. Theater budgets and government support for the arts in general have come under pressure in recent years and have limited employment prospects for costume designers. Many theaters, especially small and nonprofit theaters, are cutting their budgets or doing smaller shows that require fewer costumes. Additionally, people are less willing to spend money on tickets or go to theaters during economic downturns or times of crisis.

Nevertheless, opportunities for costume designers exist. As more cable television networks create original programming, demand for costume design in this area is likely to increase. Costume designers are able to work in an increasing number of locations as new regional theaters and cable television companies operate throughout the United States. As a result, however, designers must be willing to travel.

Competition for designer jobs is stiff and will remain so throughout the next decade. The number of qualified costume designers far exceeds the number of jobs available. This is especially true in smaller cities and regions, where there are fewer theaters.

FOR MORE INFORMATION

This union represents costume designers in film and television. For information on the industry, an article on the career, and to view costume sketches in their online gallery, check out its Web site:

Costume Designers Guild
11969 Ventura Boulevard, 1st Floor
Studio City, CA 91604-2630
Tel: 818-752-2400
Email: cdgia@costumedesignersguild.com
http://www.costumedesignersguild.com

This organization provides a list of schools, scholarships, and a journal. College memberships are available with opportunities to network among other members who are professionals in the costume field.

Costume Society of America
203 Towne Centre Drive
Hillsborough, NJ 08844-4693
Tel: 800-272-9447
Email: national.office@costumesocietyamerica.com
http://www.costumesocietyamerica.com

For additional information, contact the following organizations:

National Costumers Association
121 North Bosart Avenue
Indianapolis, IN 46201-3729
Tel: 317-351-1940
Email: office@costumers.org
http://www.costumers.org

United States Institute for Theatre Technology
6443 Ridings Road
Syracuse, NY 13206-1111
Tel: 800-938-7488
Email: info@office.usitt.org
http://www.usitt.org

This union represents many costume designers working in New York, Chicago, Los Angeles, Miami, New England, and the Mid-Atlantic. For information on membership, apprenticeship programs, and other resources on the career, contact

United Scenic Artists Local 829
29 West 38th Street
New York, NY 10018-5504
Tel: 212-581-0300
http://www.usa829.org

Creative Arts Therapists

QUICK FACTS

School Subjects
Art
Music
Theater/dance

Personal Skills
Artistic
Helping/teaching

Work Environment
Primarily indoors
Primarily one location

Minimum Education Level
Master's degree

Salary Range
$15,000 to $45,000 to
$100,000

Certification or Licensing
Recommended (certification)
Required by certain states
(licensing)

Outlook
About as fast as the average

DOT
076

GOE
14.06.01

NOC
3144

O*NET-SOC
N/A

OVERVIEW

Creative arts therapists treat and rehabilitate people with mental, physical, and emotional disabilities. They use the creative processes of music, art, dance/movement, drama, psychodrama, and poetry in their therapy sessions to determine the underlying causes of problems and to help patients achieve therapeutic goals. Creative arts therapists usually specialize in one particular type of therapeutic activity. The specific objectives of the therapeutic activities vary according to the needs of the patient and the setting of the therapy program.

HISTORY

Creative arts therapy programs are fairly recent additions to the health care field. Although many theories of mental and physical therapy have existed for centuries, it has been only in the last 75 years or so that health care professionals have truly realized the healing powers of music, art, dance, and other forms of artistic self-expression.

Art therapy is based on the idea that people who cannot discuss their problems with words must have another outlet for self-expression. In the early 1900s, psychiatrists began to look more closely at their patients' artwork, realizing that there could be links between the emotional or psychological illness and the art. Sigmund Freud even did some preliminary research into the artistic expression of his patients.

In the 1930s, art educators discovered that children often expressed their thoughts better with pictures and role-playing than they did through verbalization. Children often do not know the words they need to explain how they feel or how to make their needs known to adults. Researchers began to look into art as a way to treat children who were traumatized by abuse, neglect, illness, or other physical or emotional disabilities.

During and after World War II, the Department of Veterans Affairs (VA) developed and organized various art, music, and dance activities for patients in VA hospitals. These activities had a dramatic effect on the physical and mental well-being of World War II veterans, and creative arts therapists began to help treat and rehabilitate patients in other health care settings.

Because of early breakthroughs with children and veterans, the number of arts therapists has increased greatly over the past few decades, and the field has expanded to include drama, psychodrama, and poetry, in addition to the original areas of music, art, and dance. Today, creative arts therapists work with diverse populations of patients in a wide range of facilities, and they focus on the specific needs of a vast spectrum of disorders and disabilities. Colleges and universities offer degree programs in many types of therapies, and national associations for registering and certifying creative arts therapists work to monitor training programs and to ensure the professional integrity of the therapists working in the various fields.

THE JOB

Tapping a power related to dreaming, creative arts therapy delves into the subconscious and gives people a mode of expression in an uncensored environment. This is important because before patients can begin to heal, they must first identify their feelings. Once they recognize their feelings, they can begin to develop an understanding of the relationship between their feelings and their behavior.

The main goal of a creative arts therapist is to improve the client's physical, mental, and emotional health. Before therapists begin any treatment, they meet with a team of other health care professionals. After determining the strength, limitations, and interests of their client, they create a program to promote positive change and growth. The creative arts therapist continues to confer with the other health care workers as the program progresses, and alters the program according to the client's progress. How these goals are reached depends on the unique specialty of the therapist in question.

"It's like sitting in the woods waiting for a fawn to come out." That is how Barbara Fish, former Director of Activity Therapy for the Illinois Department of Mental Health and Developmental Disabilities, Chicago Metropolitan and Adolescent Services, describes her experience as she waits patiently for a sexually abused patient to begin to trust her. The patient is extraordinarily frightened because of the traumatic abuse she has suffered. This may be the first time in the patient's life that she is in an environment of acceptance and support. It may take months or even years before the patient begins to trust the therapist, "come out of the woods," and begin to heal.

In some cases, especially when the clients are adolescents, they may have become so detached from their feelings that they can physically act out without consciously knowing the reasons for their behavior. This detachment from their emotions creates a great deal of psychological pain. With the help of a creative arts therapist, clients can begin to communicate their subconscious feelings both verbally and nonverbally. They can express their emotions in a variety of ways without having to name them.

Creative arts therapists work with all age groups: young children, adolescents, adults, and senior citizens. They can work in individual, group, or family sessions. The approach of the therapist, however, depends on the specific needs of the client or group. For example, if an individual is feeling overwhelmed by too many options or stimuli, the therapist may give him or her only a plain piece of paper and a pencil to work with that day.

Fish has three ground rules for her art therapy sessions with disturbed adolescents: respect yourself, respect other people, and respect property. The therapy groups are limited to five patients per group. She begins the session by asking each person in the group how he or she is feeling that day. By carefully listening to their responses, a theme may emerge that will determine the direction of the therapy. For example, if anger is reoccurring in their statements, Fish may ask them to draw a line down the center of a piece of paper. On one side, she will ask them to draw how anger looks and on the other side how feeling sad looks. Then, once the drawing is complete, she will ask them to compare the two pictures and see that their anger may be masking their feelings of sadness, loneliness, and disappointment. As patients begin to recognize their true feelings, they develop better control of their behavior.

To reach their patients, creative arts therapists can use a variety of mediums, including visual art, music, dance, drama, or poetry or other kinds of creative writing. Creative arts therapists usually specialize in a specific medium, becoming a music therapist, drama therapist, dance therapist, art therapist, or poetry therapist. "In my groups we use poetry and creative writing," Fish explains. "We do all kinds of things to get at what is going on at an unconscious level."

Music therapists use musical lessons and activities to improve a patient's self-confidence and self-awareness, to relieve states of depression, and to improve physical dexterity. For example, a music therapist treating a patient with Alzheimer's might play songs from the patient's past in order to stimulate long- and short-term memory, soothe feelings of agitation, and increase a sense of reality.

Art therapists use art in much the same manner. The art therapist may encourage and teach patients to express their thoughts, feelings, and anxieties via sketching, drawing, painting, or sculpting. Art therapy is especially helpful in revealing patterns of domestic abuse in families. Children involved in such a situation may depict scenes of family life with violent details or portray a certain family member as especially frightening or threatening.

Dance/movement therapists develop and conduct dance/movement sessions to help improve the physical, mental, and emotional health of their patients. Dance and movement therapy is also used as a way of assessing a patient's progress toward reaching therapeutic goals.

There are other types of creative arts therapists as well. *Drama therapists* use role-playing, pantomime (the telling of a story by the use of expressive body or facial movements), puppetry, improvisation, and original scripted dramatization to evaluate and treat patients. *Poetry therapists* and *bibliotherapists,* use the written and spoken word to treat patients.

REQUIREMENTS
High School
To become a creative arts therapist, you will need a bachelor's degree, so take a college preparatory curriculum while in high school. You should become as proficient as possible with the methods and tools related to the type of creative arts therapy you wish to pursue. When therapists work with patients, they must be able to concentrate completely on the patient rather than on learning how to use tools or techniques. For example, if you want to become involved in art therapy, you need to be familiar with art tools (such as brushes, palette knives, etc.) as well as artistic techniques.

In addition to courses such as drama, art, music, and English, you should consider taking an introductory class in psychology. Also, a communication class will give you an understanding of the various ways people communicate, both verbally and nonverbally.

Postsecondary Training

To become a creative arts therapist, you must earn at least a bachelor's degree, usually in the area in which you wish to specialize. For example, those studying to be art therapists typically have undergraduate degrees in studio art, art education, or psychology with a strong emphasis on art courses as well.

In most cases, however, you will also need a graduate degree before you can gain certification as a professional or advance in your chosen field. Requirements for admission to graduate schools vary by program, so you would be wise to contact the graduate programs you are interested in to find out about their admissions policies. For some fields you may be required to submit a portfolio of your work along with the written application. Professional organizations can be a good source of information regarding high-quality programs. For example, both the American Art Therapy Association and the American Music Therapy Association provide lists of schools that meet their standards for approval. (Contact information for both associations is listed at the end of this article.)

In graduate school, your study of psychology and the arts field you are interested in will be in-depth. Classes for someone seeking a master's in art therapy, for example, may include group psychotherapy, foundation of creativity theory, assessment and treatment planning, and art therapy presentation. In addition to classroom study, you will also complete an internship or supervised practicum (that is, work with clients). Depending on your program, you may also need to write a thesis or present a final artistic project before receiving your degree.

Certification or Licensing

Typically, the nationally recognized association or certification board specific to your field of choice offers registration and certification. For example, the Art Therapy Credentials Board (ATCB) offers registration and certification to art therapists, and the American Dance Therapy Association offers registration to dance therapists. In general, requirements for registration include completing an approved therapy program and having a certain amount of experience working with clients. Requirements for higher levels of registration or certification generally involve having additional work experience and passing a written exam.

For a specific example, consider the certification process for an art therapist: An art therapist may receive the designation art therapist registered from the ATCB after completing a graduate program and having some experience working with clients. The next level, then, is to become a board-certified art therapist by passing a written exam. To retain certification status, therapists must complete a certain amount of continuing education.

Many registered creative arts therapists also hold additional licenses in other fields, such as social work, education, mental health, or marriage and family therapy. In some states, creative arts therapists need licensing depending on their place of work. For specific information on licensing in your field, you will need to check with your state's licensing board. Creative arts therapists are also often members of other professional associations, including the American Psychological Association, the American Association for Marriage and Family Therapy, and the American Counseling Association.

Other Requirements

To succeed in this line of work, you should have a strong desire to help others seek positive change in their lives. All types of creative arts therapists must be able to work well with other people—both patients and other health professionals—in the development and implementation of therapy programs. You must have the patience and the stamina to teach and practice therapy with patients for whom progress is often very slow because of their various physical and emotional disorders. A therapist must always keep in mind that even a tiny amount of progress might be extremely significant for some patients and their families. A good sense of humor is also a valuable trait.

EXPLORING

There are many ways to explore the possibility of a career as a creative arts therapist. Contact professional associations for information on therapy careers. Talk with people working in the creative arts therapy field and perhaps arrange to observe a creative arts therapy session. Look for part-time or summer jobs or volunteer at a hospital, clinic, nursing home, or any of a number of health care facilities.

A summer job as an aide at a camp for disabled children, for example, may help provide insight into the nature of creative arts therapy, including both its rewards and demands. Such experience can be very valuable in deciding if you are suited to the inherent frustrations of a therapy career.

EMPLOYERS

Creative arts therapists usually work as members of an interdisciplinary health care team that may include physicians, nurses, social workers, psychiatrists, and psychologists. Although often employed in hospitals, therapists also work in rehabilitation centers, nursing homes, day treatment facilities, shelters for battered women, pain and stress management clinics, substance abuse programs, hospices, and correctional facilities. Others maintain their own private practices. Many creative arts therapists work with children in grammar and high schools, either as therapists or art teachers. Some arts therapists teach or conduct research in the creative arts at colleges and universities.

STARTING OUT

After earning a bachelor's degree in a particular field, you should complete your certification, which may include an internship or assistantship. Unpaid training internships often can lead to a first job in the field. Graduates can use the career services office at their college or university to help them find positions in the creative arts therapy field. Many professional associations also compile lists of job openings to assist their members.

Creative arts therapists who are new to the field might consider doing volunteer work at a nonprofit community organization, correctional facility, or neighborhood association to gain some practical experience. Therapists who want to start their own practice can host group therapy sessions in their homes. Creative arts therapists may also wish to associate with other members of the therapy field in order to gain experience and build a client base.

ADVANCEMENT

With more experience, therapists can move into supervisory, administrative, and teaching positions. Often, the supervision of interns can resemble a therapy session. The interns will discuss their feelings and ask questions they may have regarding their work with clients. How did they handle their clients? What were the reactions to what their clients said or did? What could they be doing to help more? The supervising therapist helps the interns become competent creative arts therapists.

Many therapists have represented the profession internationally. Barbara Fish was invited to present her paper, "Art Therapy with Children and Adolescents," at the University of Helsinki. Additionally, Fish spoke in Finland at a three-day workshop exploring the use and effectiveness of arts therapy with children and adolescents. Raising the public and professional awareness of creative arts therapy is an important concern for many therapists.

EARNINGS

A therapist's annual salary depends on experience, level of training, education, and specialty. Working on a hospital staff or being self-employed also affects annual income. According to the American Art Therapy Association (AATA), entry-level art therapists earn annual salaries of approximately $32,000. Median annual salaries are about $45,000, and AATA reports that top earnings for salaried administrators ranged from $50,000 and $100,000 annually. Those who have Ph.D.s and are licensed for private practice can earn between $75 and $150 per hour, according to AATA. However those in private practice must pay professional expenses such as insurance and office rental.

Salaries for music therapists vary based on experience, level of training, and education. Music therapists earned average annual salaries of $38,816 in 2001, according to the American Music Therapy Association (AMTA). Salaries reported by AMTA members ranged from $15,000 to $100,000. According to the National Association for Music Education (MENC), music therapists earn the following annual salaries based on employment setting: hospital-psychiatric facility, $20,000 to $62,000; special education facility, $22,000 to $42,000; clinic for disabled children, $15,000 to $70,000; mental health center, $21,000 to $65,000; nursing home, $17,000 to $65,000; correctional facility, $23,000 to $58,000; and private practice, $18,000 to $77,000.

Benefits depend on the employer but generally include paid vacation time, health insurance, and paid sick days. Those who are in private practice must provide their own benefits.

WORK ENVIRONMENT

Most creative arts therapists work a typical 40-hour, five-day work-week; at times, however, they may have to work extra hours. The number of patients under a therapist's care depends on the specific employment setting. Although many therapists work in hospitals, they may also be employed in such facilities as clinics, rehabilitation centers, children's homes, schools, and nursing homes. Some therapists maintain service contracts with several facilities. For instance, a therapist might work two days a week at a hospital, one day at a nursing home, and the rest of the week at a rehabilitation center.

Most buildings are pleasant, comfortable, and clean places in which to work. Experienced creative arts therapists might choose to be self-employed, working with patients in their own studios. In such a case, the therapist might work more irregular hours to accommodate patient schedules. Other therapists might maintain a combination of service contract work with one or more facilities in addition to a private caseload of clients referred to them by other health care professionals. Whether therapists work on service contracts with various facilities or maintain private practices, they must deal with all of the business and administrative details and worries that go along with being self-employed.

OUTLOOK

The American Art Therapy Association notes that art therapy is a growing field. Demand for new therapists is created as medical professionals and the general public become aware of the benefits gained through art therapies. Although enrollment in college therapy programs is increasing, new graduates are usually able to find jobs. In cases where an individual is unable to find a full-time position, a therapist might obtain service contracts for part-time work at several facilities.

The American Music Therapy Association predicts a promising future for the field of music therapy. Demand for music therapists will grow as medical professionals and the general public become aware of the benefits gained through music therapy.

Job openings in facilities such as nursing homes should continue to increase as the elderly population grows over the next few decades. Advances in medical technology and the recent practice of early discharge from hospitals should also create new opportunities in managed care facilities, chronic pain clinics, and cancer care facilities. The demand for therapists of all types should continue to increase as more people become aware of the need to help disabled patients in creative ways. Some drama therapists and psychodramatists are also finding employment opportunities outside of the usual health care field. Such therapists might conduct therapy sessions at corporate sites to enhance the personal effectiveness and growth of employees.

FOR MORE INFORMATION

For more detailed information about your field of interest, contact the following organizations:

American Art Therapy Association
5999 Stevenson Avenue
Alexandria, VA 22304-3304
Tel: 888-290-0878
Email: info@arttherapy.org
http://www.arttherapy.org

American Dance Therapy Association
2000 Century Plaza, Suite 108
10632 Little Patuxent Parkway
Columbia, MD 21044-6258
Tel: 410-997-4040
Email: info@adta.org
http://www.adta.org

American Music Therapy Association
8455 Colesville Road, Suite 1000
Silver Spring, MD 20910-3392
Tel: 301-589-3300
Email: info@musictherapy.org
http://www.musictherapy.org

Art Therapy Credentials Board
3 Terrace Way, Suite B
Greensboro, NC 27403-3660
Tel: 877-213-2822
Email: atcb@ubcc.org
http://www.atcb.org

National Association for Drama Therapy
15 Post Side Lane
Pittsford, NY 14534-9410
Tel: 585-381-5618
Email: answers@nadt.org
http://www.nadt.org

National Association for Poetry Therapy
c/o Center for Education, Training & Holistic Approaches
777 East Atlantic Avenue, #243
Delray Beach, FL 33483-5360
Tel: 866-844-6278
Email: info@poetrytherapy.org
http://www.poetrytherapy.org

For an overview of the various types of art therapy, visit the NCCATA Web site:
National Coalition of Creative Arts Therapies Associations (NCCATA)
c/o AMTA
8455 Colesville Road, Suite 1000
Silver Spring, MD 20910-3392
http://www.nccata.org

INTERVIEW

Libby Schmanke is an instructor in the graduate art therapy program at Emporia State University in Emporia, Kansas. (Visit http://www. emporia.edu/psyspe/arttherapy/athp.html to learn more about the program.) She discussed art therapy and her program with the editors of Careers in Focus: Art.

Q. Please tell us about your background and your program.

A. My background is in substance abuse counseling. After many years in that field, I first heard about graduate art therapy training and earned my master's from Emporia State University (ESU). I was then asked to stay and become a half-time faculty member. Meantime, I have opened a private practice and studio in art therapy and creativity groups, where I am able to pursue my own painting as well. I greatly enjoy all facets of my work!

ESU offers a master of science in art therapy, which is a two-year degree housed in the Department of Psychology. Undergraduate students at Emporia State may take course work that leads to a pre–art therapy undergraduate degree, commonly a bachelor of arts in art with a minor in psychology. In the art therapy master's program, students take both art therapy and psychology course work, complete 750 hours of internship in art therapy, perform art therapy research, and complete a master's project or thesis.

Q. What is one thing that young people may not know about a career in art therapy?

A. Many people don't know that there is a distinct profession of art therapy and that entry level to the professional field is the master's degree. Many good colleges and universities offer undergraduate course work in art therapy, but professional registration, board certification, and state licensure require the master's degree. Students with an undergrad art therapy degree might find work as activity directors in nursing homes or community recreation centers. Employers seeking art therapists are looking for the master's degree.

Q. What types of students pursue art therapy study in your program?

A. At ESU, we seem to attract an equal number of students whose undergraduate focus is psychology or counseling (with an interest in art) as we do fine art students (with an interest in helping others, or a personal experience of healing). They may have seen an art exhibit on art as healing, or a television show or Web site about art therapy that inspired them. We often hear an applicant say, "When I saw . . . , I realized this is what I want to do!" At any rate, certain art and psychology courses in the undergraduate degree are needed for entry to any art therapy graduate program.

Q. What are the most important personal and professional qualities for art therapy majors?

A. Like other psychotherapists or counselors, persons interested in art therapy should like working with people. They should understand that this work involves caring, yet keeping professional boundaries, and helping the person become empowered to help themselves. Patience and the ability to set aside personal prejudices are a must for any therapist. In addition, art therapists must be interested in and knowledgeable of a variety of artistic media in both two and three dimensions. At the same time, they should understand that the process of self-expression through art-making is the focus of art therapy, not the creation of a "good" piece of art. Students who are the best artists are not necessarily the best art therapists.

Q. What is the employment outlook for the field? Have certain areas of this field been especially promising in recent years?

A. Art therapy is becoming better known all the time both here in the states and throughout the world. In certain areas of this country, the job outlook is better than others; some states license art therapists while others do not, which can be a consideration. In the early days of the field, art therapists were found primarily in inpatient psychiatric settings; nowadays, residential youth centers, schools, domestic violence shelters, hospices, prisons, substance abuse centers, outpatient mental health centers, and medical settings have art therapists on staff. Art therapy has been shown to be especially effective with survivors of trauma, and in recent years art therapists have been deployed to disaster relief settings around the world; work with returning Iraqi war veterans is another up-and-coming area of employment.

Education Directors
and Museum Teachers

QUICK FACTS

School Subjects
Art
Art history
Speech

Personal Skills
Communication/ideas
Helping/teaching

Work Environment
Primarily indoors
One location with some
travel

Minimum Education Level
Bachelor's degree

Salary Range
$18,000 to $40,000 to
$56,969+

Certification or Licensing
None available

Outlook
More slowly than the average

DOT
099

GOE
12.03.04

NOC
5124

O*NET-SOC
N/A

OVERVIEW

Museums are visited by people who come to learn and observe. *Education directors,* or *curators of education,* are responsible for helping these people enrich their visits. Education directors plan, develop, and administer educational programs at museums and other similar institutions. They plan tours, lectures, and classes for individuals, school groups, and special interest groups.

Museum teachers are hired by directors to provide information, share insight, and offer explanations of exhibits. Direct communication ranges from informal explanations at staff previews of a new exhibit, to addressing corporate donor groups, to aiding groups of schoolchildren. Museum teachers may write exhibit labels, prepare catalogs, or contribute to multimedia installations. Museum teachers also teach by demonstration, conducting studio classes or leading field trips.

HISTORY

Museums were at first private collections designed for the enjoyment of collectors and experts only. In the 18th and 19h centuries, museums were reconceived as public institutions. As public museums grew, so did their need for education directors. As Americans and Europeans began to encourage universal education, museums began to draw in uneducated visitors, resulting in the need for teaching about their collections.

In the United States, early museums displayed objects relating to science and colonial history. Some were in former homes of wealthy colonists and others were established at the first U.S. universities and colleges. In these early museums, curators or archivists maintained the collections and also explained them to visitors. As the collections grew and more visitors came, education directors and museum teachers were hired by the curators to coordinate and run educational programs.

The Pennsylvania Academy of the Fine Arts was founded in 1805 by Charles Willson Peale, William Rush, and other artists. It was the first art museum and art school in the United States. Today, there are thousands of art museums located throughout the United States. Education directors and museum teachers play a key role in informing the public about exhibits and museum programs.

THE JOB

Education directors carry out the educational goals of a museum or other similar institution. The educational goals of most of these institutions include nurturing curiosity and answering questions of visitors, regardless of age or background. Education directors work with administrators and museum boards to determine the scope of their educational programs. Large museums may offer full schedules of classes and tours, while smaller ones may only provide tours or lectures at the request of a school or other group.

Education directors plan schedules of courses to be offered through the museum. They may hire professors from local colleges or universities as well as regular educational staff members to lead tours or discussion groups. Education directors are usually responsible for training the staff members and may also work with professionals or university faculty to determine the content of a particular lecture, class, or series of lectures. They prepare course outlines and establish the credentials necessary for those who will teach the courses.

In smaller institutions the education director may do much of the teaching, lecturing, or tour leading. In museums, the education director's job often depends on the museum's collection. In art museums, for example, the education director may plan programs for older children that allow them to explore parts of the collection at their own pace.

Education directors may promote their programs on local radio or television or in newspapers. They may speak to community or school groups about the museum's education department and encourage the groups to attend. Sometimes, education directors deliver lectures or offer classes away from the museum.

The education director is responsible for the budget for all educational programs. Directors prepare budgets and supervise the records of income and spending. Often, schools or other groups are charged lower rates for tours or classes at museums. Education directors work with resource coordinators to establish budgets for resource materials. These need to be updated regularly in most institutions. The education director may also prepare grant proposals or help with fund-raising efforts for the museum's educational program. Once a grant has been received or a large gift has been offered to the education department, the education director plans for the best use of the funds within the department.

Education directors often work with exhibit designers to help create informative displays for visitors. They may also work with illustrators to produce illustrations or signs that enhance exhibits.

Education directors train their teachers, other staff members, and volunteers to work with individual visitors and groups. Some volunteers may be trained to assist teachers in presentations or to help large groups on tours. It is the responsibility of the director to see that the educational program is helpful and interesting to all visitors to the museum.

Special activities planned by education directors vary widely depending on the institution. Film programs, field trips, lectures, and full-day school programs may be offered weekly, monthly, or annually.

In larger museums, education directors may have a staff of teachers. Museum teachers may serve as *docents* or *interpreters* who interact directly with visitors. Docents also give prepared talks or provide information in a loosely structured format, asking and answering questions informally. Substantial knowledge of the exhibition's content is required, as well as sensitivity to visitor group composition and the ability to convey information to different types of audiences. Scholarly researchers, for example, have a different knowledge base and attention span than children.

Other museum teachers, such as *storytellers*, may be self-employed people who contract with a museum to provide special programs a few times a year. Many teachers are volunteers or part-time workers.

Education specialists are experts in a particular field, which may be education itself or an area in which the museum has large holdings, such as Asian textiles, Pop Art, or pre-Columbian pottery. Education specialists divide their time between planning programs and direct teaching. They may supervise other teachers, conduct field trips, or teach classes in local schools as part of joint programs of study between museums and schools.

Educational resource coordinators are responsible for the collection of education materials used in the educational programs. These may include slides, posters, videotapes, books, or materials for special projects. Educational resource coordinators prepare, buy, catalog, and maintain all of the materials used by the education department. They sometimes have a lending library of films, videos, DVDs, books, or slides that people may borrow. Resource coordinators keep track of the circulation of materials. They may also lead tours or workshops for schoolteachers or administrators to teach them about the collection of the museum and to keep them apprised of new materials that could be used in their own classrooms.

Finally, education directors and teachers attend conventions and school meetings to promote their institution's educational program and to encourage participation in their classes or tours.

REQUIREMENTS

High School

As an education director or a museum teacher, you will need a diverse educational background to perform well in your job. At the high school level, you should take courses in creative writing, literature, history, the sciences, foreign languages, art, and speech. These courses will give you general background knowledge you can use to interpret collections, write letters to school principals, design curriculum materials, develop multicultural education, and lecture to public audiences. Math and computer skills are also strongly recommended. You will use these skills when preparing budgets and calculating the number of visitors that can fit in an exhibit space, and when writing grants or asking corporations and federal agencies for program funding.

Postsecondary Training

In order to be an education director or museum teacher, you must have a bachelor's degree. Many museums also require a master's degree. The largest museums prefer to hire education directors and teachers who have doctoral degrees.

Some colleges in the United States offer programs of instruction leading to a degree in museology (the study of museums). Most education directors and teachers work in museums that specialize in art, history, or science. These professionals often have degrees in fields related to the museum's specialty. Education directors and teachers who work in more specialized museums often have studied such specialized fields as early American art, woodcarvings, or the history of abstract expressionism.

Because of their teaching duties, museum teachers and education specialists must also have a bachelor's degree in an academic discipline or in education.

Other Requirements

Excellent communication skills are essential in this field. Your primary responsibility will be to interpret and present collections to a broad public audience. The ability to motivate and teach many individuals from a wide range of cultural backgrounds, age groups, and educational levels is necessary. You should also be organized and flexible. You will be at a great advantage if you know a foreign language, sign language, and first aid.

EXPLORING

If you are interested in becoming an education director or museum teacher, volunteer experience should be easy to obtain. Most museums have student volunteers. You can request a position in the education department, where you may help with school tours, organize files or audiovisual materials, or assist a lecturer in a class.

College-preparatory courses are important if you are interested in this field. Apply to colleges or universities with strong liberal arts programs. Courses in art, history, science, and education are recommended if you want to work at museums. Some larger museums offer internships to college students who are interested in the field.

The American Association of Museums publishes an annual museum directory, a monthly newsletter, and a bimonthly magazine. It also publishes *Careers in Museums: A Variety of Vocations. Introduction to Museum Work,* published by the American Association for State and Local History, discusses the educational programs at various museums. (See the end of this article for contact information.)

EMPLOYERS

Institutions with a primary goal to educate the public about their collections hire education directors and teachers. Depending on each institution's monetary resources, most museums, large and small, and occasionally historical societies, employ education directors and teachers to ensure public access to their collections. Institutions with small operating budgets or limited visitor access sometimes hire part-time educators or rely on volunteer support.

STARTING OUT

Your first job in a museum will likely be as a teacher or resource coordinator working in the education department. With a few years of experience and improved understanding of the institution's collection, you may enter competition for promotion to education director. Many people in the field transfer from one museum to another.

ADVANCEMENT

Once in the education department, most people learn much of their work on the job. Experience in working with different people and groups becomes very important. Education directors must continually improve their understanding of their own institution's collection so that they can present it to school and other groups in the best way possible. Some education directors work for the federal government in specific subject areas such as art, aeronautics, science, or technology. They must be proficient in these fields as well as in education.

Museum teachers with experience and appropriate academic or teaching credentials may become content specialists in one area of the museum's collection or may become a director of education, assuming responsibility for the departmental budget, educational policies and community outreach programs, and training and supervision of numerous staff and volunteer workers. Advancement may depend on acquisition of an advanced degree in education or in an academic field. Because professional supervisory positions are few in comparison to the number of teacher positions, museum teachers may need to look beyond their home institution for advancement opportunities, perhaps accepting a smaller salary at a smaller museum in return for a supervisory title.

Teachers who leave museum work are well positioned to seek employment elsewhere in the nonprofit sector, especially with grant-funding agencies involved in community-based programs. In the for-profit sector, excellent communication skills and the ability to express an institution's philosophy both in writing and in interviews are skills valued by the public relations departments of corporations.

EARNINGS

According to Salary.com, 50 percent of education specialists who were employed at museums earned between $36,389 and $49,739 in 2007. Salaries ranged from less than $31,463 to $56,969 or more annually. Museum teachers can expect to earn from $18,000 to $22,000 to start. Those with experience earn from $25,000 to $35,000 or more. Fringe benefits, including medical and dental insurance, paid vacations and sick leave, and retirement plans, vary according to each employer's policies.

WORK ENVIRONMENT

People who choose to be education directors and teachers enjoy spending time in museums. They also enjoy teaching, planning activities, organizing projects, and carrying a great deal of responsibility. Those in museums may like the quiet of an art museum or the energy and life of a science museum aimed at children. Directors and teachers should enjoy being in an academic environment where they work closely with scholars and researchers.

Education directors in larger institutions usually have their own offices where they do planning and other administrative work, but they spend the majority of their time in other parts of the museum and at other locations where they lead education programs.

Most museum teachers have a base of operation in the museum but may not have a private office, since the bulk of their work is carried out in exhibit areas, in resource centers or study rooms within the museum, in classrooms outside of the museum, or in the field. Permanent staff members work a normal workweek, with occasional weekend or evening assignments.

OUTLOOK

Employment for education directors and museum teachers is expected to increase more slowly than the average for all occupations through the next decade. Budget cutbacks have affected many museums and other cultural institutions, which have in turn reduced the size of their education departments.

Many educators with specialties in the arts and other fields are interested in becoming education directors at museums. Competition is especially intense for positions in large cities and in institutions with more prestigious reputations. Some smaller museums may cut out their education director position altogether until the economic climate improves, or they may get by with part-time staff.

FOR MORE INFORMATION

For a directory of museums and other information, contact
American Association of Museums
1575 Eye Street, NW, Suite 400
Washington, DC 20005-1113
Tel: 202-289-1818
http://www.aam-us.org

Fashion Designers and Illustrators

QUICK FACTS

School Subjects
Art
Family and consumer science

Personal Skills
Artistic
Communication/ideas

Work Environment
Primarily indoors
One location with some travel

Minimum Education Level
Some postsecondary training

Salary Range
$30,000 to $62,610 to
$117,120+ (designers)
$18,350 to $41,970 to
$79,390+ (illustrators)

Certification or Licensing
None available

Outlook
More slowly than the
average (designers)
About as fast as the average
(illustrators)

DOT
141

GOE
01.04.02 (designers)
01.04.01 (illustrators)

NOC
5243 (designers)
5241 (illustrators)

O*NET-SOC
27-1022.00 (designers)
27-1013.00 (illustrators)

OVERVIEW

Fashion designers create or adapt original designs for clothing for men, women, and children. Most specialize in one particular type of clothing, such as women's dresses or men's suits. Most designers work for textile, apparel, and pattern manufacturers. Some designers are self-employed and develop a clientele of individual customers or manufacturers. Others work for fashion salons, high-fashion department stores, and specialty shops. A few work in the entertainment industry, designing costumes.

Fashion illustrators are illustrators whose artistic focus is specifically on styles of clothing and personal image. Illustrators use a variety of media (for example, pencil, pen and ink, or computer technology) to create illustrations that appear in print and electronic formats.

There are approximately 17,000 fashion designers and 29,000 fine artists (which includes a small number of fashion illustrators) employed in the United States.

HISTORY

Originally, people wore garments to help them maintain body temperature rather than for style. Clothing usually was handmade at home. Dress design became a profession around the 1600s. Before the invention of the sewing machine in 1846 by Elias Howe, all garments were made by hand. One of the first designers was Rose Bertin, a French milliner (creator of fashion accessories such as hats and cloaks) who dressed Marie Antoinette and influenced women's fashions before and during the French Revolution.

Women dominated dress design until 1858, when Charles Frederick Worth, an English tailor and couturier of Empress Eugenie, consort of Napoleon III, opened a salon, or fashion house, in Paris. There, he produced designs for actresses and other wealthy clients—the only individuals with enough time and money to have clothing created specifically for them. Worth was the first designer to make garments from fabrics he had selected; until that time, dressmakers had used fabrics provided by patrons. Worth also was the first designer to display his creations on live models. Today, French designers continue to dominate the field. However, the U.S. garment industry has assumed a position of leadership in clothing design and production in the last 40 years, as London and Milan also have become important fashion centers.

Illustration figured prominently in the ancient civilizations of Mesopotamia, Egypt, and later Greek and Roman civilizations. Drawings depicting knowledge and conveying ideas have also been found among ancient Assyrian, Babylonian, Egyptian, and Chinese societies. Modern illustration began during the Renaissance of the 15th and 16th centuries, with the work of Leonardo da Vinci, Andreas Vesalius, and Michelangelo Buonarotti.

Over time, tools have been developed to aid illustrators in their work. Illustrators have made use of parallel bars, compasses, French curves, and T squares, but the development of computer technology has largely replaced these mechanical tools with software such as computer-aided design. Today, fashion illustrators combine their artistic skill with technology to produce illustrations that appear in such diverse places as magazines, billboards, and Web sites.

THE JOB

Fashion designers create designs for almost anything that is a part of the costume of men, women, or children. They design both outer and inner garments, hats, purses, shoes, gloves, costume jewelry, scarves, or beachwear. Some specialize in certain types of clothing, such as bridal gowns or sportswear. People in this profession range from the few top *haute couture designers* who produce one-of-a-kind designs for high-fashion firms, called houses, to the thousands of designers who create fashions for mass production and sale to millions of Americans. The largest number of fashion designers are followers rather than originators of fashion, adapting high-end styles to meet the desires of the general public. Many fashion designers are self-employed; some work on a freelance basis.

The designer's original idea for a garment is usually sketched. After a rough sketch is created, the designer begins to shape the pattern pieces that make the garment. The pieces are drawn to actual size on paper and cut out of a rough material, often muslin. The muslin pieces are sewn together and fitted on a model. The designer makes modifications in the pattern pieces or other features of the rough mock-up to complete the design. From the rough model, sample garments are made from the fabric that the designer intends to use.

Today's designers are greatly assisted by computer software. Computer-aided designing and computer-aided manufacturing allow for thousands of fashion styles and colors to be stored in a computer and accessed at the touch of a button, largely eliminating the long process of gathering fabrics and styling them into samples.

Sample garments are displayed at a "showing," to which press representatives and buyers are invited to see the latest designs. Major designers may present large runway shows twice a year to leading retailers and the fashion press for potential publicity and sales. Sample garments may then be mass-produced, displayed by fashion models, and shipped to stores where they are available for purchase.

In some companies, designers are involved in every step of the production of a selected line, from the original idea to the completed garments. Many designers prefer to supervise their own workrooms. Others work with supervisors to solve problems that arise in the production of the garments.

Most manufacturers produce new styles four times each year: spring and summer; fall and winter; vacation wear, and holiday styles. Designers generally are expected to create between 50 and 150 styles for each showing. Their work calendar differs from the actual time of year. They must be working on spring and summer designs during fall and winter, and on fall and winter clothing during the summer, so as to prepare for future season's fashion production.

Designers work cooperatively with the head of their manufacturing firm. They design a line that is consistent with the ideas of their employers. They also work cooperatively with those who do the actual production of the garments and must be able to estimate the cost of a garment. Some company designers produce designs and oversee a workroom staff, which may consist of a *head designer*, an *assistant designer*, and one or more *sample makers*. Designers in large firms may plan and direct the work of one or more assistant designers, select fabrics and trims, and help determine the pricing of the products they design.

Designers spend time in exploration and research, visiting textile manufacturing and sales establishments to learn of the latest fabrics and their uses and capabilities. They must know about fabric, weave, draping qualities, and strength of materials. A good understanding of textiles and their qualities underlies much of designers' work. They browse through stores to see what fashion items are being purchased by the public and which are passed by. They visit museums and art galleries to get ideas about color and design. They go to places where people congregate—theaters, sports events, business and professional meetings, and resorts—and meet with marketing and production workers, salespeople, and clients to discover what people are wearing and to discuss ideas and styles.

Designers also keep abreast of changing styles. If the styles are too different from public taste, customers will probably reject the designs. If, however, they cling to styles that have been successful in the past, they may find that the taste of buyers has changed dramatically. In either case, it could be equally disastrous for their employers.

There are many opportunities for specialization in fashion designing. The most common specialties are particular types of garments such as resort wear, bridalwear, or sportswear.

An interesting specialty in fashion designing is theatrical design, a relatively limited field but challenging to those who are interested in combining an interest in theater with a talent for clothing design.

Fashion illustrators can work in any of several different areas of the fashion field. They provide artwork to accompany editorial pieces in magazines such as *Glamour, Redbook,* and *Seventeen* and newspapers such as *Women's Wear Daily.* Catalog companies employ fashion illustrators to provide the artwork that sells their merchandise through print or online publications.

Fashion illustrators also work with fashion designers, editors, and models. They make sketches from designers' notes or they may sketch live models during runway shows or other fashion presentations. They may use pencils, pen and ink, charcoal, paint, airbrush, computer technology, or a combination of media.

While illustrators must be artistically talented (able to visualize designs, use colors, and create style), they must also be adept at using technologies such as digital cameras and various computer programs designed to manipulate illustrations and photographs.

Fashion illustrators may work as freelancers, handling all the business aspects that go along with being self-employed. Such

Fashion designers must have strong communication skills. *(Gareth Brown, Corbis)*

responsibilities include keeping track of expenses, billing clients promptly and appropriately, and keeping their businesses going by lining up new jobs for when a current project ends.

Because the fashion world is extremely competitive and fast-paced, fashion illustrators tend to work long hours under the pressure of deadlines and demanding personalities.

REQUIREMENTS

High School

A high school diploma is needed for fashion designing and illustrating and should include courses that prepare you for more specialized training after graduation. Art (including drawing), home economics, mathematics, and chemistry should all be included.

Postsecondary Training

An aspiring designer with a total fashion background that includes marketing and other business skills will be favored by employers over a talented person with no knowledge of business procedures. A college degree is recommended, although not required. Graduation from a fashion design school is highly desirable. Employers seek designers who have completed courses in mathematics, business, design, sketching, art history, costume history, literature, pattern making, clothing construction, and textiles.

Some colleges offer a four-year degree in fine arts with a major in fashion design. Many reputable schools of fashion design offer a two- or three-year program that offers a diploma or certificate.

Students interested in fashion should take computer-aided design courses, as computers are increasingly being used by designers to better visualize a final product, create prototypes, and reduce design production time and cost. Companies are looking for more than design skills, many require extensive knowledge and experience with software programs used to produce technical drawings.

Although you don't need to take a specific postsecondary educational route to become a fashion illustrator, there are a number of options available to you. There are, for example, academic programs in fashion illustration at many colleges, universities, and adult education centers. Some community and junior colleges offer associate's degrees in commercial art. An advantage to pursuing education beyond high school is that it gives you an opportunity to build a portfolio, which is a collection of an artist's best sketches that shows prospective clients a variety of skills. In addition to studying art and photography, it is advantageous to study clothing construction, fabrics, fashion design, or cosmetology.

Other Requirements

Prospective fashion designers and illustrators must be artistic and imaginative with a flair for color and clothing coordination. They will need a working knowledge of clothing construction and an eye for trends. They must possess technical aptitudes, problem-solving skills, and the ability to conceptualize in two and three dimensions.

Personal qualifications include self-motivation, team spirit, and the ability to handle pressure, deadlines, and long hours. These careers also demand energy and a good head for business.

EXPLORING

If you enjoy sewing, you may have taken the first step toward exploring a career in fashion design. If your skills in garment construction are adequate, the next step may be an attempt at designing and making clothing. Art and design courses will help assess your talent and ability as a creative artist.

If you are able to obtain a summer job in a department or specialty store, you can observe retailing practices and gain some practical insights into the merchandising aspects of the fashion world. Working in a fabric store can provide the opportunity to learn about fabrics and accessories. You may want to visit a garment manufacturer to see fashion employees at work.

You can explore the world of illustration by taking drawing classes both at school and through local organizations such as community centers. Also, consider joining a school art club. These clubs will give you the opportunity to meet with others who share your interests, and they sometimes sponsor talks or meetings with professionals. Try drawing or sewing your own fashion creations. If you can't find work at a camera or art store, try getting a job at a clothing store. This will give you experience working with people and clothes, and you might even be able to suggest fashion advice to customers.

Aspiring designers and illustrators can also attend style shows, visit art galleries, observe clothing worn by fashion leaders, and browse through a variety of stores in which garments are sold. Many useful books and magazines are published about fashion. The so-called fashion industry bible is *Women's Wear Daily,* a must-read for those who want to be knowledgeable and current in this fast-changing business. For subscription information, visit http://www.wwd.com.

EMPLOYERS

Approximately 17,000 fashion designers are employed in the United States. Many fashion designers find employment with large fashion houses such as Liz Claiborne or Jones New York. Some large manufacturers produce a secondary line of lower-priced designer clothing—Donna Karan's DKNY and Giorgio Armani's Emporio, for example. In the United States, New York City, San Francisco, and Los Angeles are major fashion centers and positions may be found in both large and small companies. Work also may be found in Chicago and other cities, although not as many jobs are available in these locations.

A few fashion designers work for high-fashion firms, but these positions are difficult to come by and competition is very strong. An aspiring designer may have more options in specialized areas of fashion such as sportswear, sleepwear, children's clothing, or accessories.

Other areas for aspiring fashion designers to explore are home fashions such as bed and bath linens, draperies, and rugs or carpeting. Positions also can be found with pattern manufacturers. Some fashion designers work on a freelance basis, contracting with manufacturers or individuals.

An easy way to learn about manufacturers is to visit a department or specialty store and examine labels and tags on merchandise of interest. In addition to major department stores, other retailers such as Target carry a variety of manufacturers' lines.

There are approximately 29,000 fine artists (which includes a small number of fashion illustrators) employed in the United States. More than 60 percent of all visual artists (which includes illustrators) are self-employed. Others work for large retailers, magazines, newspapers, design or advertising firms, and fashion houses.

STARTING OUT

Few people begin their careers as fashion designers. Well-trained college graduates often begin as assistant designers. Assistants must prove their ability before being entrusted with the responsible job of the designer. Many young people find that assistant designer jobs are difficult to locate, so they accept beginning jobs in the workroom where they spend time cutting or constructing garments.

Fashion design school graduates may receive placement information from their school or college career services offices. Approaching stores and manufacturers directly is another way to secure a beginning position. However, you will be more successful if you have contacts in the industry through previous summer or part-time work.

Illustrators sometimes start out receiving no pay for their work, just a byline (a credit giving the person's name). However, having your name published with your work will give you exposure on a professional level. As you take on more work, you may be able to begin charging more. Again, it may take some time to become established in the field.

ADVANCEMENT

Advancement in fashion designing varies a great deal. There is much moving from firm to firm, and vacancies occur frequently. Aspiring designers should create, collect, and continuously update their portfolios of designs and look for opportunities to show their work to employers. Beginners may work as cutting assistants or assistant designers. From these entry-level positions, the fashion designer's career path may lead to positions as an assistant technical designer, pattern company designer, designer, and head designer. Those who grow with a company may design less and take on more operational responsibilities.

Designers may choose to move into a business or merchandising position where they direct lines, set prices, supervise production, and work directly with buyers. After years of work, top designers may become partners in the design or apparel firms for which they work. Others may open their own retail clothing stores. A designer may want to work for firms that offer increasing design responsibility and fewer restrictions to become established as a house designer or eventually as an independent-name designer.

Advancement for fashion illustrators generally comes as they gain professional recognition. The freelance illustrator who becomes known for the creativity and high quality of his or her work will find that he or she has a growing clientele. More clients translate into more jobs; more jobs translate into higher earnings. In addition, as illustrators become better known, they can charge more for their services and be more selective about what jobs they take. Illustrators who are salaried employees of organizations may either move up within the organization, taking on supervisory roles or working with specific accounts for example, or they may have starting their own illustration business as their ultimate goal.

EARNINGS

Fashion designers earned an average annual salary of $62,610 in 2006, according to the U.S. Department of Labor. The lowest paid 10 percent earned less than $30,000; the highest paid 10 percent earned more than $117,120. A few highly skilled and well-known designers in top firms have annual incomes of over $150,000. Top fashion designers who have successful lines of clothing can earn bonuses that bring their annual incomes into the millions. As designers become well known, they are usually offered a share of the ownership of the company for which they design. Their ownership percentage increases with their reputation.

Theatrical designers usually work on a contract basis. Although the compensation for the total contract is usually good, there may be long periods of idleness between contracts. The annual incomes for theatrical designers usually are not as great as those of fashion designers, although while they are working they may be making more than $1,000 per week.

The U.S. Department of Labor reports that median earnings for salaried fine artists, including painters, sculptors, and illustrators, were $41,970 a year in 2006. The top 10 percent earned more than $79,390 and the bottom 10 percent earned less than $18,350.

Illustrators running their own businesses and working on a freelance basis are typically paid by the job. The pay for these jobs may be based on such factors as the illustrator's reputation, the prestige of the client (for example, a fashion magazine with an international readership will pay more than a local newspaper doing a Sunday fashion spread), and the difficulty of the work. For some of this work, illustrators may make $250 per job. They may also get credit lines and receive travel expenses. Freelance illustrators who have national or international reputations may make in the hundreds of thousands of dollars or more per year. Freelance workers, unlike salaried artists, however, do not have benefits such as health insurance and paid vacation or sick days.

WORK ENVIRONMENT

Fashion design is competitive and stressful, but often exciting and glamorous. Many designers work in cluttered and noisy surroundings. Their work environment may consist of a large room with long tables for cutting out patterns or garments. There may be only one or two other people working in the room, or there may be several other workers. Many designers travel a great deal for showings and conferences. They may spend time in stores or shops looking at clothing that has been manufactured by competitors.

Most designers work a 40-hour week, but they may have to work more during rush periods. Styles previewed for one season require a great amount of work during the weeks and months before a show. The work pace is usually hectic as pressure builds before collection showings.

Although fashion illustrators typically have well-lighted, organized work spaces with room to accommodate their tools, they are also in a fast-paced, deadline-driven environment. Illustrators may often need to put in long or irregular hours to complete an assignment to a client's satisfaction. Freelance illustrators have the added pressure of continually seeking new clients and uncertain incomes. Establishing oneself in the field can take years, and this is also a stressful process. On the positive side, fashion illustrators are able to enjoy working in creative environments where visual images are highly valued.

OUTLOOK

Designers are key people in the garment industry, yet relatively few of them are needed to make employment possible for thousands of people in other apparel occupations. It is estimated that fashion designers in the United States constitute less than 1 percent of the garment industry. Some designers work only for the high-priced custom trade, some for the mass market, and some on exclusive designs that will be made for only one person. Many designers are employed by manufacturers of paper patterns.

Some fashion designers enjoy high pay and prestige. Those at the top of their profession rarely leave their positions. Therefore, opportunities for newcomers are limited. There always will be more people hoping to break into the field than there are available jobs. Experience working with computer-aided design programs is increasingly important to employers and can help to distinguish a qualified job candidate from the rest of his or her competition. Employment prospects may be better in specialized areas, such as children's clothing. Additionally, openings are more readily available for assistant designers. According to the *Occupational Outlook Handbook,* employment of designers is expected to grow more slowly than the average for all occupations through 2014. However, increasing populations and growing personal incomes are expected to continue to create demand for the most talented fashion designers.

Employment for visual artists (including illustrators) is expected to grow as fast as the average for all occupations through 2014, according to the U.S. Department of Labor. For illustrators specifically working in fashion, employment will likely be dependent on the prosperity of agencies involved with the fashion field, such as magazines, newspapers, advertising firms, and fashion houses. The outlook for these agencies currently looks strong. The popularity of American fashions around the world should create a demand for illustrators. In addition, numerous outlets for fashion, such as e-zines and retail Web sites, will create a need for illustrators. Competition for jobs, however, will be keen since these positions are highly attractive to people with artistic ability. In addition, the *Occupational Outlook Handbook* notes that the growing popularity of computer art programs can allow consumers and businesses to produce and access illustrations on their own. Despite this improved technology, the specialized skills of the trained illustrator should still find demand in the fashion world. Individuals who are creative and persistent in finding job leads and who are able to adapt to rapidly changing technologies will be the most successful.

FOR MORE INFORMATION

For industry information, contact
Council of Fashion Designers of America
1412 Broadway, Suite 2006
New York, NY 10018-9250
http://www.cfda.com

Those interested in creating men's fashions should visit the CTDA Web site for business and training information.
Custom Tailors and Designers Association of America (CTDA)
PO Box 41331
Cleveland, OH 44141-0331
Tel: 888-248-2832
Email: info@ctda.com
http://www.ctda.com

For information about this school, its programs, and an application, contact FIT.
Fashion Institute of Technology (FIT)
Seventh Avenue at 27th Street
New York, NY 10001-5992
Tel: 212-217-7999
Email: fitinfo@fitnyc.edu
http://www.fitnyc.edu

This organization is committed to improving conditions for all creators of graphic art and to raising standards for the entire industry.
Graphic Artists Guild
32 Broadway, Suite 1114
New York, NY 10004-1612
Tel: 212-791-3400
http://www.gag.org

For industry information, contact
International Association of Clothing Designers & Executives
835 Northwest 36th Terrace
Oklahoma City, OK 73118-7104

Tel: 405-602-8037
http://www.iacde.com

For a list of accredited schools, contact
National Association of Schools of Art and Design
11250 Roger Bacon Drive, Suite 21
Reston, VA 20190-5248
Tel: 703-437-0700
Email: info@arts-accredit.org
http://nasad.arts-accredit.org

This national institution promotes and stimulates interest in the art of illustration by offering exhibits, lectures, educational programs, and social interchange.
Society of Illustrators
128 East 63rd Street
New York, NY 10021-7303
Tel: 212-838-2560
Email: info@societyillustrators.org
http://www.societyillustrators.org

For subscription information, visit this magazine's Web site.
Women's Wear Daily
http://www.wwd.com

Gallery Owners and Directors

OVERVIEW

Gallery owners are entrepreneurs who start or buy their own for-profit or nonprofit art gallery. They are responsible for all aspects of a business operation, from working with artists to overseeing day-to-day operations. *Gallery directors* are responsible for the profitable management and operation of art galleries.

HISTORY

The Louvre, which is considered by many to be the first art gallery or museum in the world, was established in Paris, France, in 1793. It gave the general public its first opportunity to view works of fine art—thereby starting a trend toward public appreciation of art.

Galleries were also established by individuals as an extension of their personal interests and love of art and antiques. For example, Sir John Soane, an English architect who specialized in the neoclassical style, purchased a house in London, England, in 1792 and used it as his residence, but also to entertain clients. Between 1794 and 1824, Soane remodeled and expanded the property, gradually filling it with great works of art and architecture. He eventually bequeathed his house and collection, now known as Sir John Soane's Museum, to the British people.

Throughout the 1800s and 1900s, public and private art galleries were built throughout the United States and the world. Most large cities and towns established galleries to display their artistic treasures and help educate the public about art. Academic institutions also began establishing galleries. These galleries were typically linked with the schools' art departments and offered educational and cultural opportunities to the surrounding community. Galleries were also established by wealthy individuals who were interested in giving back to their communities. As more galleries were founded, it soon became clear that highly educated professionals were needed to manage their day-to-day operations—hence the career of gallery director was born.

THE JOB

Gallery directors are responsible for every phase of a gallery's operation. They often are one of the first employees to arrive in the morning and the last to leave at night. The duties of gallery directors vary according to the type of art sold (if it is a for-profit gallery), the size of the gallery, and the number of employees. Their duties include working with artists and the public; researching and organizing exhibitions; writing catalog or brochure copy for exhibitions; setting up exhibitions; hiring, training, and supervising employees; maintaining the physical surroundings of the gallery; hosting gallery tours; selling artwork (at for-profit galleries); monitoring expenditures and receipts; fund-raising (at nonprofit galleries); corresponding with clients and artists; and marketing the gallery and its artists to the public (including writing press releases, being interviewed by the media, and updating the gallery's Web site). In small galleries, directors may handle all of these tasks. In large galleries that employ more staff, however, directors may be involved in only a few of these activities.

Gallery owners, especially those who own smaller galleries that are not managed by a gallery director, perform many or all of the aforementioned duties. They typically work longer hours based on the fact they have to do all the tasks that a normal business owner has to do (such as payroll, hiring and supervising employees, budgeting for new acquisitions to the gallery, collecting payments) in addition to showing artwork.

Owners and directors should be good at working with all different kinds of people. Differences of opinion and personality clashes among employees are inevitable; therefore, they must be able to restore good feelings among the staff. Owners and directors may have to deal with difficult or upset customers, and must attempt to restore goodwill toward the gallery when customers are dissatisfied.

REQUIREMENTS

High School

You will need at least a high school diploma in order to become a gallery owner or director. Helpful courses include art, history, business, mathematics, marketing, and economics. English and speech classes are also important. These courses will teach you to communicate effectively with all types of people, including artists, employees, and customers. Studying a foreign language may also be helpful.

Gallery owners need patience and fortitude to overcome the slow times and other challenges involved in operating a business. (Tom Stewart, Corbis)

Postsecondary Training

You do not need a college degree to work as a gallery owner or director, but a degree or at least some postsecondary education will certainly give you an advantage over other applicants in this highly competitive field. Many owner and directors have degrees in art, art history, marketing, history, or business management. College courses that will help you prepare for a career as a gallery owner or director include art theory, art administration, art history, accounting, business, marketing, English, advertising, and computer science. All owners and directors, regardless of their education, must have good marketing, analytical, communication, and people skills.

Certification or Licensing

A business license may be a requirement in some states. Individual states or communities may have zoning codes or other regulations specifying what type of business can be located in a particular area. Check with your state's chamber of commerce or department of revenue for more information on obtaining a license, or visit http://www.sba.gov/hotlist/license.html.

Other Requirements

Gallery professionals need a lot of energy, patience, and fortitude to overcome the slow times and other difficulties involved in owning and/or running a business. Other important personal characteristics include maturity, creativity, and good business judgment.

Gallery owners and managers should also have good communication skills and enjoy working with and supervising others. They also should be able to motivate employees and delegate authority. Diplomacy often is necessary when dealing with artists.

EXPLORING

High school activities that may give you useful experience include forming and managing an art club. You could also volunteer as a docent at a local art museum or apply for an internship at a local gallery. Ask your art teacher to help you arrange an information interview with a gallery owner or director.

EMPLOYERS

Art galleries are located throughout the United States. They range from large, taxpayer-funded galleries such as the National Gallery of Art in Washington, D.C., to university-run galleries such as the

Yale University Art Gallery, to private galleries in small towns that specialize in the work of a handful of local artists.

STARTING OUT

Few people start their careers as gallery owners or directors. Many start as *gallery assistants*, *art consultants*, or *assistant directors* or in some other position in the art industry. If you attend college, an internship at an art gallery is an excellent way to learn about these careers and make valuable contacts. Your college's career services offices will also be useful for finding job leads.

ADVANCEMENT

Gallery owners don't advance in the same manner as gallery directors or other gallery workers. Instead, they might "advance" by getting the opportunity to display more prestigious works of art or by opening additional galleries or expanding their existing gallery. Some gallery owners become renowned for their knowledge about the art world and are sought out by members of the media to offer commentary on developments in the field.

Advancement opportunities for gallery directors vary according to the size, reputation, and location of the gallery and the interests of the director. Advancement also depends on the individual's work experience and educational background. Some directors may decide to open their own galleries after they have acquired enough experience. Others may work as writers, art consultants, and educators.

EARNINGS

Earnings for gallery owners vary widely and are greatly influenced by the abilities of the individual owner, the type of gallery (nonprofit or for-profit), the type and volume of art being sold, and existing economic conditions. Some gallery owners may earn less than $15,000 a year, while the most successful owners earn $100,000 or more.

Salaries for gallery directors depend on the size, type, and reputation of the gallery and the director's job responsibilities. A director employed by a well-known gallery in New York, Chicago, or Boston typically earns more than a director employed at a gallery in a small town or rural area. Directors at commercial galleries usually earn higher salaries than those directors who are employed by nonprofit galleries. The U.S. Department of Labor categorizes the career of gallery director under the general heading of "retail manager." In 2006, these professionals had median annual earnings of $33,960. Salaries ranged from less than $21,420 to $59,710 or more annually.

Gallery directors typically receive full benefits, including health insurance, paid vacation, and sick leave.

WORK ENVIRONMENT

Most art galleries are pleasant, intellectually engaging places to work, and owners and directors often have comfortable offices. Most art galleries are open five or more days a week. They are typically open during regular business hours, but many offer extended hours in the evening. Owners and directors often work as many as 50 to 60 hours a week.

Some gallery owners and directors may travel to visit artists' studios, attend auctions, or participate in museum/art history conferences.

OUTLOOK

The careers of gallery owner and gallery director are much-sought-after positions in the art world. As a result, competition for these jobs will be very strong over the next decade. Applicants with strong educational backgrounds, comprehensive knowledge of art, and extensive work experience will have the best chances of finding jobs.

FOR MORE INFORMATION

For art resources and listings of galleries, contact
Art Dealers Association of America
575 Madison Avenue
New York, NY 10022-2511
Tel: 212-940-8590
http://www.artdealers.org

This organization represents directors of the major art museums in North America. It sells a publication on professional practices, a salary survey, and a sample employment contract.
Association of Art Museum Directors
120 East 56th Street, Suite 520
New York, NY 10022-3673
Tel: 212-754-8084
http://www.aamd.org

For information on art galleries nationwide and special events, contact

Fine Art Dealers Association (FADA)
PO Box 2953
Carmel, CA 93921-2953
http://www.fada.com

INTERVIEW

Ken Saunders is a partner in Marx-Saunders Gallery, LTD (http://www.marxsaunders.com) in Chicago, Illinois. He discussed his career with the editors of Careers in Focus: Art.

Q. Please describe a day in your life as an art dealer.

A. I spend a large portion of each day on routine administrative duties. The more successful the gallery, the more complex the business of running the gallery becomes. For each exhibition a press release, a show announcement, and catalogue are created. Photographs are collected from the artist, an essay is commissioned, a designer is consulted. The show announcement is sent out to 2,000 collectors, the artist's accommodations need to be arranged. A preview is planned and invitations are created and mailed out for that event. The catalogue is mailed to 650 collectors around the world. Reservations and catering is arranged. The previous exhibition ends and is de-installed, the new work arrives (we show sculpture and dealing with large fragile objects is a challenge to say the least), and it must be installed and lit.

There are phone calls. We represent 25 artist and we speak to them each between two and 20 times a month each.

There are bills to pay. Insurance claims to chase. Museum loans, art fairs, payroll, taxes, and payroll taxes. Collectors: We drop everything for them. Tourists: We drop everything for them, too. Ten-hour days on our feet. (Glamorous!)

Q. Tell us about the travel that is involved for your job.

A. As I mentioned earlier, we do a number of art fairs each year. We spend about seven days in the venue city. The days are very long and even though there is a lot of moneymaking and important development going on it doesn't feel very glamorous.

Our artists live around the world. About once every five years we try to pay a visit to each. They often live in very rural areas.

Q. How did you train for this career?

A. I was an artist in college. My undergraduate degree is in poetry. After school I curated art shows at night clubs, published a literary magazine, and mounted a reading series at art galleries.

When I was 25 I got a job selling memberships at The Art Institute of Chicago. Later that year I got a part-time job at an art gallery. After several promotions I was offered a partnership in the gallery. After 10 years of selling paintings, Bonnie Marx offered me a partnership in Marx-Saunders Gallery, LTD.

Q. What advice would you give to high school students who are interested in this career?

A. Polish your communication skills. Dealing art is a sales job. I am not a museum curator; I am a small business owner. Art dealers are very independent; nonetheless, "people skills" are going to be essential.

This is glamorous work (on good days). But it is hard work. The customer is always right, and no one apologizes as well as I apologize. This is very personal work; we become very close to our artists and to our collectors. For better or for worse! As the owner of the gallery, I have built a lot of flexibility into my personal schedule. Although I work Saturdays (this can take a lot of getting used to), I do feel like I can make time for my family as needed.

Graphic Designers

OVERVIEW

Graphic designers are practical artists whose creations are intended to express ideas, convey information, or draw attention to a product. They design a wide variety of materials, including advertisements, displays, packaging, signs, computer graphics and games, book and magazine covers and interiors, animated characters, and company logos to fit the needs and preferences of their various clients. There are approximately 228,000 graphic designers employed in the United States.

HISTORY

The challenge of combining beauty, function, and technology in whatever form has preoccupied artisans throughout history. Graphic design work has been used to create products and promote commerce for as long as people have used symbols, pictures, and typography to communicate ideas.

Graphic design grew alongside the growth of print media (newspapers, magazines, catalogs, and advertising). Typically, the graphic designer would sketch several rough drafts of the layout of pictures and words. After one of the drafts was approved, the designer would complete a final layout including detailed type and artwork specifications. The words were sent to a typesetter and the artwork assigned to an illustrator. When the final pieces were returned, the designer or a keyline and paste-up artist would adhere them with rubber cement or wax to an illustration board. Different colored items were placed on acetate overlays. This camera-ready art was now ready to be sent to a printer for photographing and reproduction.

QUICK FACTS

School Subjects
Art
Computer science

Personal Skills
Artistic
Communication/ideas

Work Environment
Primarily indoors
Primarily one location

Minimum Education Level
Some postsecondary training

Salary Range
$20,000 to $44,000 to
$100,000+

Certification or Licensing
None available

Outlook
About as fast as the average

DOT
141

GOE
01.04.02

NOC
5241

O*NET-SOC
27-1024.00

Computer technology has revolutionized the way many graphic designers do their work. Today it is possible to be a successful graphic designer even if you can't draw more than simple stick figures. Graphic designers are now able to draw, color, and revise the many different images they work with using computers. They can choose typefaces, size type, and place images without having to manually align them on the page using a T square and triangle. Computer graphics enable graphic designers to work more quickly, since details like size, shape, and color are easy to change.

Graphics design programs are continually revised and improved, moving more and more design work from the artist's table to the computer mousepad and graphics tablet. As computer technology continues to advance in the areas of graphics and multimedia, more designers will have to know how to work with virtual reality applications.

THE JOB

Graphic designers are not primarily fine artists, although they may be highly skilled at drawing or painting. Most designs commissioned to graphic designers involve both artwork and copy (words). Thus, the designer must not only be familiar with the wide range of art media (photography, drawing, painting, collage, etc.) and styles, but he or she must also be familiar with a wide range of typefaces and know how to manipulate them for the right effect. Because design tends to change in a similar way to fashion, designers must keep up-to-date with the latest trends. At the same time, they must be well grounded in more traditional, classic designs.

Graphic designers can work as *in-house designers* for a particular company, as *staff designers* for a graphic design firm, or as *freelance designers* working for themselves. Some designers specialize in designing advertising materials or packaging. Others focus on corporate identity materials such as company stationery and logos. Some work mainly for publishers, designing book and magazine covers and page layouts. Some work in the area of computer graphics, creating still or animated graphics for computer software, videos, or motion pictures. A highly specialized type of graphic designer, the *environmental graphic designer,* designs large outdoor signs. Depending on the project's requirements, some graphic designers work exclusively on the computer, while others may use both the computer and drawings or paintings created by hand.

Whatever the specialty and whatever the medium, all graphic designers take a similar approach to a project, whether it is for an entirely new design or for a variation on an existing one. Graphic designers begin by determining the needs and preferences of clients and potential users, buyers, or viewers.

For example, if a graphic designer is working on a company logo, he or she will likely meet with company representatives to discuss such points as how and where the company is going to use the logo and what size, color, and shape preferences company executives might have. Project budgets must be respected: A design that may be perfect in every way but that is too costly to reproduce is basically useless. Graphic designers may need to compare their ideas with similar ones from other companies and analyze the image they project. They must have a good knowledge of how various colors, shapes, and layouts affect the viewer psychologically.

After a plan has been conceived and the details worked out, the graphic designer does some preliminary designs (generally two or three) to present to the client for approval. The client may reject the preliminary designs entirely and request a new one, or he or she may ask the designer to make alterations. The designer then goes back to the drawing board to attempt a new design or make the requested changes. This process continues until the client approves the design.

Once a design has been approved, the graphic designer prepares the piece for professional reproduction, or printing. The printer may require what is called a mechanical, in which the artwork and copy are arranged on a white board just as it is to be photographed, or the designer may be asked to submit an electronic copy of the design. Either way, designers must have a good understanding of the printing process, including color separation, paper properties, and halftone (photograph) reproduction.

REQUIREMENTS

High School
While in high school, take any art and design courses that are available. Computer classes are also helpful, particularly those that teach page layout programs or art and photography manipulation programs. Working on the school newspaper or yearbook can provide valuable design experience. You could also volunteer to design flyers or posters for school events.

Postsecondary Training
More graphic designers are recognizing the value of formal training; at least two out of three people entering the field today have a college degree or some college education. About 250 colleges and art

schools offer art and graphic design programs that are accredited by the National Association of Schools of Art and Design. At many schools, graphic design students must take a year of basic art and design courses before being accepted into the bachelor's degree program. In addition, applicants to the bachelor's degree programs in graphic arts may be asked to submit samples of their work to prove artistic ability. Many schools and employers depend on samples, or portfolios, to evaluate the applicants' skills in graphic design.

Many programs increasingly emphasize the importance of using computers for design work. Computer proficiency will be very important in the years to come. Interested individuals should select an academic program that incorporates computer training into the curriculum, or train themselves on their own.

A bachelor of fine arts program at a four-year college or university may include courses such as principles of design, art and art history, painting, sculpture, mechanical and architectural drawing, architecture, computer design, basic engineering, fashion designing and sketching, garment construction, and textiles. Such degrees are desirable but not always necessary for obtaining a position as a graphic designer.

Other Requirements

As with all artists, graphic designers need a degree of artistic talent, creativity, and imagination. They must be sensitive to beauty, have an eye for detail, and have a strong sense of color, balance, and proportion. Many of these qualities come naturally to potential graphic designers, but skills can be developed and improved through training, both on the job and in professional schools, colleges, and universities.

More and more graphic designers need solid computer skills and working knowledge of several of the common drawing, image editing, and page layout programs. Graphic design can be done on both Macintosh systems and on PCs; in fact, many designers have both types of computers in their studios.

With or without specialized education, graphic designers seeking employment should have a good portfolio containing samples of their best work. The graphic designer's portfolio is extremely important and can make a difference when an employer must choose between two otherwise equally qualified candidates.

A period of on-the-job training is expected for all beginning designers. The length of time it takes to become fully qualified as a graphic designer may run from one to three years, depending on prior education and experience, as well as innate talent.

On the Web

About: Art History
http://arthistory.about.com

About: Drawing/Sketching
http://drawsketch.about.com

The American Museum of Photography
http://www.photographymuseum.com

The Art Institute of Chicago: Art Access
http://www.artic.edu/artaccess

ArtCyclopedia
http://artcyclopedia.com

ArtisanCam
http://www.artisancam.org.uk

Artist Resource: Job Hunting Advice for Designers, Artists, and Illustrators
http://www.artistresource.org/jobhunt.htm

Artists Foundation: Resources for Artists
http://www.artistsfoundation.org/art_pages/resources/resources.htm

ArtSchools.com
http://www.artschools.com

FanArtReview.com
http://www.fanartreview.com

GradSchools.com: Art and Fine Arts
http://www.gradschools.com/art_fine.html

Metropolitan Museum of Art
http://www.metmuseum.org

National Endowment for the Arts
http://www.nea.gov

Smithsonian American Art Museum
http://nmaa-ryder.si.edu

WorldArtPortfolio.com
http://www.worldartportfolio.com

Yahoo: Arts
http://dir.yahoo.com/arts

EXPLORING

If you are interested in a career in graphic design, there are a number of ways to find out whether you have the talent, ambition, and perseverance to succeed in the field. Take as many art and design courses as possible while still in high school and become proficient at working on computers. To get an insider's view of various design occupations, you could enlist the help of art teachers or school guidance counselors to make arrangements to tour design firms and interview designers.

While in school, seek out practical experience by participating in school and community projects that call for design talents. These might include such activities as building sets for plays, setting up exhibits, planning seasonal and holiday displays, and preparing programs and other printed materials. If you are interested in publication design, work on the school newspaper or yearbook is invaluable.

Part-time and summer jobs are excellent ways to become familiar with the day-to-day requirements of a design job and gain some basic related experience. Possible places of employment include design studios, design departments in advertising agencies and manufacturing companies, department and furniture stores, flower shops, workshops that produce ornamental items, and museums. Museums also use a number of volunteer workers. Inexperienced people are often employed as sales, clerical, or general assistants; those with a little more education and experience may qualify for jobs in which they have a chance to develop actual design skills and build portfolios of completed design projects.

EMPLOYERS

Graphic designers hold approximately 228,000 jobs. They work in many different industries, including the wholesale and retail trade (such as department stores, furniture and home furnishings stores, apparel stores, and florist shops); manufacturing industries (such as machinery, motor vehicles, aircraft, metal products, instruments, apparel, textiles, printing, and publishing); service industries (such as business services, engineering, and architecture); construction firms; and government agencies. Public relations and publicity firms, advertising agencies, and mail-order houses all have graphic design departments. The publishing industry is a primary employer of graphic designers, including book publishers, magazines, newspapers, and newsletters.

About 30 percent of all graphic designers are self-employed, a higher proportion than is found in most other occupations. These freelance designers sell their services to multiple clients.

STARTING OUT

The best way to enter the field of graphic design is to have a strong portfolio. Potential employers rely on portfolios to evaluate talent and how that talent might be used to fit the company's needs. Beginning graphic designers can assemble a portfolio from work completed at school, in art classes, and in part-time or freelance jobs. The portfolio should continually be updated to reflect the designer's growing skills so it will always be ready for possible job changes.

Those just starting out can apply directly to companies that employ designers. Many colleges and professional schools have career services offices to help graduates find positions, and sometimes it is possible to get a referral from a previous part-time employer or volunteer coordinator.

ADVANCEMENT

As part of their on-the-job training, beginning graphic designers generally are given simpler tasks and work under direct supervision. As they gain experience, they move up to more complex work with increasingly less supervision. Experienced graphic designers, especially those with leadership capabilities, may be promoted to chief designer, design department head, or other supervisory positions.

Graphic designers with strong computer skills can move into other computer-related positions with additional education. Some may become interested in graphics programming in order to further improve computer design capabilities. Others may want to become involved with multimedia and interactive graphics. Video games, touch-screen displays in stores, and even laser light shows are all products of multimedia graphic designers.

When designers develop personal styles that are in high demand in the marketplace, they sometimes go into business for themselves. Freelance design work can be erratic, however, so usually only the most experienced designers with an established client base can count on consistent full-time work.

EARNINGS

The range of salaries for graphic designers is quite broad. Many earn as little as $20,000, while others make more than $100,000. Salaries depend primarily on the nature and scope of the employer. The U.S. Department of Labor reports that in 2006, graphic designers earned a median salary of $39,900; the highest paid 10 percent earned $69,730 or more, while the lowest paid 10 percent earned $24,120 or less.

The American Institute of Graphic Arts/Aquent Salary Survey 2007 reports that designers earned a median salary of $44,000, while senior designers earned a median of $60,000 annually. Salaried designers who advance to the position of creative/design director earned a median of $90,000 a year.

Self-employed designers can earn a lot one year and substantially more or less the next. Their earnings depend on individual talent and business ability, but, in general, are higher than those of salaried designers. However, like any self-employed individual, freelance designers must pay their own insurance costs and taxes and are not compensated for vacation or sick days.

Graphic designers who work for large corporations receive full benefits, including health insurance, paid vacation, and sick leave.

WORK ENVIRONMENT

Most graphic designers work regular hours in clean, comfortable, pleasant offices or studios. Conditions vary depending on the design specialty. Some graphic designers work in small establishments with few employees; others work in large organizations with large design departments. Some deal mostly with their coworkers; others may have a lot of public contact. Freelance designers are paid by the assignment. To maintain a steady income, they must constantly strive to please their clients and to find new ones. At times, graphic designers may have to work long, irregular hours in order to complete an especially ambitious project.

OUTLOOK

Employment for qualified graphic designers is expected to grow about as fast as the average for all occupations through 2014; employment should be especially strong for those involved with computer graphics and animation. As computer graphic and Web-based technology continues to advance, there will be a need for well-trained computer graphic designers. Companies that have always used graphic designers will expect their designers to perform work on computers. Companies for which graphic design was once too time-consuming or costly are now sprucing up company newsletters and magazines, among other things, requiring the skills of design professionals.

Because the design field appeals to many talented individuals, competition is expected to be strong in all areas. Beginners and designers with only average talent or without formal education and technical skills may encounter some difficulty in finding a job.

FOR MORE INFORMATION

For more information about careers in graphic design, contact
American Institute of Graphic Arts
164 Fifth Avenue
New York, NY 10010-5901
Tel: 212-807-1990
http://www.aiga.org

Visit the NASAD's Web site for information on schools.
National Association of Schools of Art and Design (NASAD)
11250 Roger Bacon Drive, Suite 21
Reston, VA 20190-5248
Tel: 703-437-0700
Email: info@arts-accredit.org
http://nasad.arts-accredit.org

If you are interested in working in environmental design, contact
Society for Environmental Graphic Design
1000 Vermont Avenue, NW, Suite 400
Washington, DC 20005-4921
Tel: 202-638-5555
Email: segd@segd.org
http://www.segd.org

To read an online newsletter featuring competitions, examples of top designers' work, and industry news, visit the SPD Web site.
Society of Publication Designers (SPD)
17 East 47th Street, 6th Floor
New York, NY 10017-1920
Tel: 212-223-3332
Email: mail@spd.org
http://www.spd.org

Illustrators

QUICK FACTS

School Subjects
Art
Computer science

Personal Skills
Artistic
Following instructions

Work Environment
Primarily indoors
Primarily one location

Minimum Education Level
High school diploma

Salary Range
$18,350 to $41,970 to
$79,390+

Certification or Licensing
Voluntary

Outlook
About as fast as the average

DOT
141

GOE
01.04.01

NOC
5241

O*NET-SOC
27-1013.00, 27-1013.01

OVERVIEW

Illustrators prepare drawings for advertisements, magazines, books, newspapers, packaging, Web sites, computer programs, and other formats. *Medical illustrators,* with special training in biology and the physical sciences, are able to draw accurate illustrations of parts of the human body, animals, and plants. *Fashion illustrators* specialize in distinctive illustrations of the latest women's and men's fashions. *Natural science illustrators* create illustrations of plants and wildlife, often for museums. *Children's book illustrators* create artwork for books and other publications for young people.

HISTORY

The history of illustration can be traced back to the 8th century. Several famous illuminated manuscripts were created in the Middle Ages, including the *Book of Kells*. In the 15th century, movable type was introduced and came to be used by book illustrators. Other printing methods such as etching, woodcuts, and copper engravings were used as illustration techniques in the 16th century and beyond.

In 1796, lithography was invented in Germany. In the original process of lithography, artists made prints directly from designs drawn on slabs of stone. Metal sheets eventually replaced these stone slabs. By the mid-1800s, illustrators used lithographs and engravings to draw magazine and newspaper pages.

As knowledge of photography developed and advanced reproduction processes were invented, artists increasingly used photographs as illustrations. Many industries today, ranging from advertising to fashion, employ illustrators.

THE JOB

Illustrators create artwork for both commercial and fine art purposes. They use a variety of media—pencil, pen and ink, pastels, paints (oil, acrylic, and watercolor), airbrush, collage, and computer technology. Illustrations are used to decorate, describe, inform, clarify, instruct, and draw attention. They appear everywhere in print and electronic formats, including books, magazines, newspapers, signs and billboards, packaging (for everything from milk cartons to CDs), Web sites, computer programs, greeting cards, calendars, stationery, and direct mail.

Illustrators often work as part of a creative team, which can include graphic designers, photographers, and individuals who draw lettering called *calligraphers*. Illustrators work in almost every industry. Medical illustration and fashion illustration are two of the fastest growing specialties.

Medical illustrators use graphics, drawings, and photographs to make medical concepts and descriptions easier to understand. They provide illustrations of anatomical and biological structures and processes, as well as surgical and medical techniques and procedures. Their work is found in medical textbooks, magazines and journals, advertisements for medical products, instructional films and videotapes, television programs, exhibits, lectures and presentations, and computer-assisted learning programs. Some medical illustrators create three-dimensional physical models, such as anatomical teaching models, models used for teaching medical procedures, and also prosthetics.

Medical illustrators generally work with physicians, surgeons, biologists, and other scientists. When detailing a surgical procedure, they may observe the surgeon during surgery, and take instruction and advice from the surgeon about which parts of an operation to illustrate. They may illustrate parts of the body—the eye, the skeletal structure, the muscular structure, the structure of a cell, for example—for textbooks, encyclopedias, medical product brochures, and related literature. They may work with researchers to identify new organisms, develop new drugs, and examine cell structures, illustrating aspects of the researchers' work. They may also assist in developing sophisticated computer simulations, which allow physicians in training to "perform" a surgical procedure entirely on a computer before they are skilled enough to operate on actual patients. Medical illustrators also animate physical, biological, and anatomical processes for films and videotapes.

A medical illustrator may work in a wide range of medical and biological areas or specialize in a particular area, such as cell

An illustrator uses computer technology to create an illustration.
(Evan Hurd, Corbis)

structure, blood, disease, or the eye. Much of their work is done with computers; however, they must still have strong skills in traditional drawing and drafting techniques.

Fashion illustrators work in a glamorized, intense environment. Their artistic focus is specifically on styles of clothing and personal image. Illustrators can work in a few different categories of the fashion field. They provide artwork to accompany editorial pieces in magazines such as *Glamour, Redbook,* and *Vogue* and newspapers such as *Women's Wear Daily.* Catalog companies employ fashion illustrators to provide the artwork that sells their merchandise.

Fashion illustrators also work with fashion designers, editors, and models. They make sketches from designers' notes or they may sketch live models during runway shows or other fashion presentations. They may use pencils, pen and ink, charcoal, paint, or a combination of media. Fashion illustrators may work as freelancers, handling all the business aspects that go along with being self-employed.

Natural science illustrators create illustrations of plants and wildlife. They often work at museums such as the Smithsonian Institution.

Children's book illustrators are illustrators who specialize in creating artwork for books and other publications for young people.

REQUIREMENTS

High School

Creative talent is more important in this field than education. However, there are academic programs in illustration at most colleges and universities. If you are considering going on to a formal program, be sure to take plenty of art classes while in high school. Elective classes in illustration, ceramics, painting, or photography are common courses offered at many high schools.

Postsecondary Training

To find a salaried position as a general illustrator, you should have at least a high school diploma and preferably an associate's or bachelor's degree in commercial art or fine art. Whether you are looking for full-time employment or freelance assignments, you will need an organized collection of samples of your best work, which is called a portfolio. Employers are especially interested in work that has been published or printed. An advantage to pursuing education beyond high school is that it gives you an opportunity to build your portfolio.

Medical illustrators are required to earn a bachelor's degree in either biology or art and then complete an advanced degree program in medical illustration. These programs usually include training in traditional illustration and design techniques, computer illustration, two- and three-dimensional animation, prosthetics, medical computer graphics, instructional design and technology, photography, motion media production, and pharmaceutical advertising. Course work will also include pharmacology, basic sciences including anatomy and physiology, pathology, histology, embryology, neuroanatomy, and surgical observation and/or participation.

Graduate-level certificate programs in natural science illustration are available for aspiring natural science illustrators, with training in field sketching and botanical and zoological illustration. Fashion illustrators should study clothing construction, fashion design, and cosmetology in addition to taking art courses. They should also keep up with the latest fashion and illustration trends by reading fashion magazines.

Certification or Licensing

Illustrators need to continue their education and training while pursuing their careers. Licensing and certification are not required in this field. However, illustrators must keep up with the latest innovations in design techniques, computer software, and presentation technology, as well as technological advances in the fields for which they provide illustrations.

Most medical illustrators are members of the Association of Medical Illustrators (AMI). The AMI helps to establish accreditation and curriculum standards, offers certification in medical illustration, and provides other educational and support services to members and prospective members of this profession.

Other Requirements
Illustrators must be creative, and, of course, demonstrate artistic talent and skill. They also need to be flexible. Because their art is often commercial in nature, illustrators must be willing to accommodate their employers' desires if they are to build a broad clientele and earn a decent living. They must be able to take suggestions and rejections gracefully.

EXPLORING

You can explore an interest in this career by taking art courses. Artists can always improve their drawing skills by practicing on their own, either producing original artwork, or making sketches from drawings that appear in textbooks and reference manuals that relate to their interests. Participation in art, science, and fashion clubs is also good exposure.

EMPLOYERS

More than 60 percent of all visual artists are self-employed. Illustrators who are not self-employed work in advertising agencies, design firms, commercial art and reproduction firms, or printing and publishing firms. They are also employed in the motion picture and television industries, wholesale and retail trade establishments, and public relations firms.

Medical illustrators are employed at hospitals, medical centers, schools, laboratories, pharmaceutical companies, medical and scientific publishers, and advertising agencies. Fashion illustrators are employed at magazines, newspapers, and catalog companies. Natural science illustrators are often employed by museums, zoos, aquariums, magazines, and publishing houses. Children's books illustrators are employed by publishing houses.

STARTING OUT

Graduates of illustration programs should develop a portfolio of their work to show to prospective employers or clients. Most schools offer career counseling and job placement assistance to their graduates. Job ads and employment agencies are also potential sources for locating work.

Books to Read

Blackman, Cally. *100 Years of Fashion Illustration*. London, U.K.: Laurence King Publishing, 2007.

Edwards, Betty. *New Drawing on the Right Side of the Brain Workbook*. New York: Penguin Group, 2002.

Fleishman, Michael. *Starting Your Career as a Freelance Illustrator or Graphic Designer*. New York: Allworth Press, 2001.

Gordon, Barbara. *Opportunities in Commercial Art and Graphic Design Careers*. New York: McGraw-Hill, 2003.

Heller, Steven, and Marshall Arisman. *Inside the Business of Illustration*. New York: Allworth Press, 2004.

Hodges, Elaine R.S., et al. *The Guild Handbook of Scientific Illustration*. 2d ed. Hoboken, N.J.: John Wiley & Sons, 2003.

Lee, Jennifer B., and Miriam Mandelbaum. *Seeing Is Believing: 700 Years of Scientific and Medical Illustration*. New York: New York Public Library, 1999.

Parramon's Editorial Team. *All About Techniques in Illustration*. Hauppauge, N.Y.: Barron's, 2001.

Pope, Alice (ed). *2008 Children's Writer's & Illustrator's Market*. Cincinnati, Ohio: Writers Digest Books, 2007.

Reed, Walt. *The Illustrator in America, 1860-2000*. 3d ed. New York: Collins Design, 2003.

Slade, Catharine. *The Encyclopedia of Illustration Techniques*. Philadelphia: Running Press, 1997.

Medical illustrators can also find job placement assistance with the AMI. In addition to the job leads, AMI also provides certification that is often preferred by employers.

ADVANCEMENT

After an illustrator gains experience, he or she will be given more challenging and unusual work. Those with strong computer skills will have the best chances for advancement. Illustrators can advance by developing skills in a specialized area, or even starting their own business. Illustrators can also go into teaching in colleges and universities at the undergraduate and graduate levels.

EARNINGS

The pay for illustrations can be as little as a byline, though in the beginning of your career it may be worth it just to get exposure. Some illustrators can earn several thousand dollars for a single illustration. Freelance work is often uncertain because of the fluctuation in pay rates and steadiness of work. The U.S. Department of Labor reports that median earnings for salaried fine artists, including painters, sculptors, and illustrators, were $41,970 a year in 2006. The top 10 percent earned more than $79,390 and the bottom 10 percent earned less than $18,350.

Illustrators generally receive good benefits, including health and life insurance, pension plans, and vacation, sick, and holiday pay. Self-employed illustrators must take care of their own benefits.

WORK ENVIRONMENT

Illustrators generally work in clean, well-lit offices. They spend a great deal of time at their desks, whether in front of a computer or at the drafting table. Medical illustrators are sometimes required to visit operating rooms and other health care settings while natural science illustrators may be required to sketch subjects in their natural habitat. Fashion illustrators may be required to attend fashion shows and other industry events. Because the fashion world is extremely competitive and fast-paced, fashion illustrators tend to work long hours under the pressure of deadlines and demanding personalities.

OUTLOOK

Employment of visual artists is expected to grow about as fast as the average for all occupations through 2014, according to the *Occupational Outlook Handbook*. The growth of the Internet should provide opportunities for illustrators, although the increased use of computer-aided design systems is a threat because individuals do not necessarily need artistic talent or training to use them.

The employment outlook for medical illustrators is very good. Because there are only a few graduate programs in medical illustration with small graduation classes, medical illustrators will find great demand for their skills. The field of medicine and science in general is always growing, and medical illustrators will be needed to depict new techniques, procedures, and discoveries.

The outlook for careers in fashion illustration is dependent on the businesses of magazine publishing and advertising. Growth of advertising and public relations agencies will provide new jobs. The popularity of American fashion in other parts of the world will also create a demand for fashion illustrators to provide the artwork needed to sell to a global market.

FOR MORE INFORMATION

For information on working as a botanical artist, contact
American Society of Botanical Artists
47 Fifth Avenue
New York, NY 10003-4303
Tel: 866-691-9080
http://huntbot.andrew.cmu.edu/ASBA/ASBotArtists.html

For information on certification and educational and career opportunities for medical illustrators, contact
Association of Medical Illustrators
810 East 10th Street
Lawrence, KS 66044-3018
Tel: 866-393-4264
Email: hq@ami.org
http://www.medical-illustrators.org

This organization is committed to improving conditions for all creators of graphic art and to raising standards for the entire industry. For information, contact
Graphic Artists Guild
32 Broadway, Suite 1114
New York, NY 10004-1612
Tel: 212-791-3400
http://www.gag.org

For information on membership, contact
Guild of Natural Science Illustrators
PO Box 652
Ben Franklin Station
Washington, DC 20044-0652
Tel: 301-309-1514
Email: gnsihome@his.com
http://www.gnsi.org

For information on education programs, contact
National Association of Schools of Art and Design
11250 Roger Bacon Drive, Suite 21
Reston, VA 20190-5248
Tel: 703-437-0700
Email: info@arts-accredit.org
http://nasad.arts-accredit.org

For information on membership, contact
Society of Children's Book Writers and Illustrators
8271 Beverly Boulevard
Los Angeles, CA 90048-4515
Tel: 323-782-1010
Email: scbwi@scbwi.org
http://www.scbwi.org

This organization promotes and stimulates interest in the art of illustration by offering exhibits, lectures, educational programs, and social exchange. For information, contact
Society of Illustrators
128 East 63rd Street
New York, NY 10021-7303
Tel: 212-838-2560
Email: info@societyillustrators.org
http://www.societyillustrators.org

Interior Designers and Decorators

OVERVIEW

Interior designers and *interior decorators* evaluate, plan, and design the interior areas of residential, commercial, and industrial structures. In addition to helping clients select equipment and fixtures, these professionals supervise the coordination of colors and materials, obtain estimates and costs within the client's budget, and oversee the execution and installation of the project. They also often advise clients on architectural requirements, space planning, and the function and purpose of the environment.

There are approximately 65,000 interior designers working in the United States. These specialists are employed by interior design or architectural firms, departments stores, furniture stores, hotel chains, and large corporations.

HISTORY

Appreciation for beauty has been expressed in many artforms, including music, painting, sculpture, and poetry. One way to make such beauty a part of everyday life is through decoration of the interiors of buildings. Individuals throughout history have added personal touches of decoration to their homes. Until recently, however, major design and decorating projects have been the privilege of the wealthy.

Artists such as Michelangelo were employed to design and beautify palaces and other buildings, making use of sculpture, paintings, and other wall coverings. Kings sometimes made names for themselves by the decorating trends initiated in their palaces. Such trends came to include furniture, draperies, and often clothing. Home designs and furniture were either largely functional, as in the early American tradition, or extremely ornate, as in the style of Louis XIV of France.

As our society prospered, the field of interior design emerged. While Elsie de Wolfe was the first person to actually practice interior design as a separate profession in 1905, it wasn't until the 1950s that the design revolution really began. Today, design professionals plan interiors of homes, restaurants, hotels, hospitals, theaters, stores, offices, and other buildings.

THE JOB

The terms *interior designer* and *interior decorator* are sometimes used interchangeably. However, there is an important distinction between the two. Interior designers plan and create the overall design for interior spaces, while interior decorators focus on the decorative aspects of the design and furnishing of interiors. A further distinction concerns the type of interior space on which the design or decorating professional works. Specifically, *residential designers* focus on individual homes, while *contract* or *commercial designers* specialize in office buildings, industrial complexes, hotels, hospitals, restaurants, schools, factories, and other nonresidential environments.

Interior designers and decorators perform a wide variety of services, depending on the type of project and the clients' requirements. A job may range from designing and decorating a single room in a private residence to coordinating the entire interior arrangement of a huge building complex. In addition to planning the interiors of new buildings, interior professionals also redesign existing interiors.

Design and decorating specialists begin by evaluating a project. They first consider how the space will be used. In addition to suiting the project's functional requirements, designs must address the needs, desires, tastes, and budget of the client as well. The designer often works closely with the architect in planning the complete layout of rooms and use of space. The designer's plans must work well with the architect's blueprints and comply with other building requirements. Design work of this kind is usually done in connection with the building or renovation of large structures.

Interior professionals may design the furniture and accessories to be used on a project, or they might work with materials that are already available. They select and plan the arrangement of furniture, draperies, floor coverings, wallpaper, paint, and other decorations.

They make their decisions only after considering general style, scale of furnishings, colors, patterns, flow, lighting, safety, communication, and a host of other factors. They must also be familiar with local, state, and federal laws as well as building codes and other related regulations.

Although interior designers and decorators may consult with clients throughout the conceptual phase of the design project, they usually make a formal presentation once the design has been formulated. Such presentations may include sketches, scaled floor plans, drawings, models, color charts, photographs of furnishings, and samples of materials for upholstery, draperies, and wall coverings. Designers and decorators also usually provide a cost estimate of furnishings, materials, labor, transportation, and incidentals required to complete the project.

Once plans have been approved by the client, the interior designer and decorator assembles materials—drapery fabrics, upholstery fabrics, new furniture, paint, and wallpaper—and supervises the work, often acting as agent for the client in contracting the services of craftworkers and specifying custom-made merchandise. Interior professionals must be familiar with many materials used in furnishing. They must know when certain materials are suitable, how they will blend with other materials, and how they will wear. They must also be familiar with historical periods influencing design and have a knack for using and combining the best contributions of these designs of the past. Since designers and decorators supervise the work done from their plans, they should know something about painting, carpet laying, carpentry, cabinet making, and other craft areas. In addition, they must be able to buy materials and services at reasonable prices while producing quality work.

Some designers and decorators specialize in a particular aspect of interior design, such as furniture, carpeting, or artwork. Others concentrate on particular environments, such as offices, hospitals, restaurants, or transportation, including ships, aircraft, and trains. Still others specialize in the renovation of old buildings. In addition to researching the styles in which rooms were originally decorated and furnished, these workers often supervise the manufacture of furniture and accessories to be used.

Considerable paperwork is involved in interior design and decoration, much of it related to budgets and costs. Interior professionals must determine quantities and make and obtain cost estimates. In addition, designers and decorators write up and administer contracts, obtain permits, place orders, and check deliveries carefully. All of this work requires an ability to attend to detail in the business aspect of interior design.

REQUIREMENTS

High School

Although formal training is not always necessary in the field of interior design, it is becoming increasingly important and is usually essential for advancement. Most architectural firms, department stores, and design firms accept only professionally trained people, even for beginning positions.

If you're considering a career as an interior designer or decorator, classes in home economics, art history, design, fine arts, and drafting will prove to be valuable. Since interior design is both an art and a business, such courses as marketing, advertising, accounting, management, and general business are important as well.

Postsecondary Training

Professional schools offer two- or three-year certificates or diplomas in interior design. Colleges and universities award undergraduate degrees in four-year programs, and graduate study is also available. The Council for Interior Design Accreditation (CIDA) accredits bachelor's degree programs in interior design. There are more than 145 accredited interior design programs offered through art, architecture, and home economics schools in the United States and Canada. The National Association of Schools of Art and Design also accredits colleges and universities with programs in art and design.

College students interested in entering the interior design field should take courses in art history, architectural drawing and drafting, fine arts, furniture design, codes and standards of design, and computer-aided design, as well as classes that focus on the types of materials primarily used, such as fibers, wood, metals, and plastics. Knowledge of lighting and electrical equipment as well as furnishings, art pieces, and antiques, is important.

In addition to art and industry-specific areas of study, courses in business and management are vital to aspiring interior designers and decorators. Learning research methods will help you stay abreast of government regulations and safety standards. You should also have some knowledge of zoning laws, building codes, and other restrictions. Finally, keeping up with product performance and new developments in materials and manufacture is an important part of the ongoing education of the interior designer and decorator.

Art historians, people with architecture or environmental planning experience, and others with qualifications in commercial or industrial design may also qualify for employment in interior design.

Certification or Licensing

Currently, 24 states, the District of Columbia, and Puerto Rico require licensing for interior designers, according to the U.S. Department of Labor. Each of these states has its own requirements for licensing and regulations for practice, so it's important to contact the specific state in order to find out how one can apply. To become eligible for registration or licensing in these jurisdictions, applicants must satisfy experience and education requirements and take the National Council for Interior Design Qualification (NCIDQ) examination.

To prepare students for this examination, the NCIDQ offers the Interior Design Experience Program. Participants are required to complete 3,520 hours of documented experience in the following categories: programming, schematic design, design development, contract documents, contract administration, and professional practice. According to the council, this experience may be achieved through "working directly in a competency area, by observing others who are engaged in such work, or by attending lectures, seminars, and continuing education courses." Students who have completed at least 96 semester credits hours (or 144 quarter credits hours of education) in an interior design program accredited by the Council for Interior Design Accreditation are eligible to participate.

Additionally, the National Kitchen and Bath Association offers several certifications to designers who specialize in kitchen and bath design.

Other Requirements

First and foremost, interior designers and decorators need to have artistic talent, including an eye for color, proportion, balance, and detail, and have the ability to visualize. Designers must be able to render an image clearly and carry it out consistently. At the same time, artistic taste and knowledge of current and enduring fashion trends are essential.

In addition, interior designers need to be able to supervise craftworkers and work well with a variety of other people, including clients and suppliers. Designers should be creative, analytical, and ethical. They also need to be able to focus on the needs of clients, develop a global view, and have an appreciation of diversity. Finally, precision, patience, perseverance, enthusiasm, and attention to detail are vital.

EXPLORING

If you're thinking about becoming an interior designer or decorator, there are several ways to learn about the field. Courses in home economics or any of the fine arts, offered either at school or through a local organization, can give you a taste of some of the areas of knowledge needed by interior designers.

To get a sense of the actual work done by design specialists, you may be able to find a part-time or summer job in a department or furniture store. Such experience will enable you to learn more about the materials used in interior design and decorating and to see the store's interior design service in action. Since the business aspects of interior design are just as important as the creative side, any kind of general selling or business experience will prove to be valuable. As a salesperson at any type of store, for example, you'll learn how to talk to customers, write up orders, close sales, and much more.

In addition to learning about interior design itself, knowledge of auxiliary and support industries will be useful as well. To get a firsthand look at associated fields, you may want to arrange a visit to a construction site, examine an architect's blueprints, talk to someone who specializes in lighting, or tour a furniture manufacturing plant.

Ultimately, the best way to learn about interior design or decorating is to talk to a design professional. While interviewing an interior designer or decorator will be interesting and enlightening, finding a mentor who is doing the type of work that you may want to do in the future is ideal. Such a person can suggest other activities that may be of interest to you as you investigate the interior design field, provide you with the names of trade magazines and/or books that can shed some light on the industry, and serve as a resource for questions you might have.

EMPLOYERS

Approximately 65,000 interior designers and decorators are employed in the United States. Interior designers and decorators can be found wherever there is a need to style or beautify the interior environment of a building. The main professional areas in which they work are residential, government, commercial, retail, hospitality, education and research, health care, and facilities management.

In addition to "traditional" interior design and decorating opportunities, some professionals design theater, film, and television settings. A few designers become teachers, lecturers, or consultants, while others work in advertising and journalism.

The majority of interior designers and decorators work either for themselves or for companies employing fewer than five people. Since the industry is not dominated by giant conglomerates or

An interior designer (right) studies fabrics with a client. *(Chris Carroll, Corbis)*

even mid-sized firms, employment opportunities are available all across the United States, as well as abroad, in cities both large and small.

STARTING OUT

Most large department stores and design firms with established reputations hire only trained interior designers and decorators. More often than not, these employers look for prospective employees with a good portfolio and a bachelor of fine arts degree. Many schools, however, offer apprenticeship or internship programs in cooperation with professional studios or offices of interior design. These programs make it possible for students to apply their academic training in an actual work environment prior to graduation.

After graduating from a two- or three-year training program (or a four-year university), the beginning interior professional must be prepared to spend one to three years as an assistant to an experienced designer or decorator before achieving full professional status. This is the usual method of entering the field of interior design and gaining membership in a professional organization.

Finding work as an assistant can often be difficult, so be prepared to take any related job. Becoming a sales clerk for interior furnishings, a shopper for accessories or fabrics, or even a receptionist or stockroom assistant can help you get a foot in the door and provide valuable experience as well.

ADVANCEMENT

While advancement possibilities are available, competition for jobs is intense and interior designers and decorators must possess a combination of talent, personality, and business sense to reach the top. Someone just starting out in the field must take a long-range career view, accept jobs that offer practical experience, and put up with long hours and occasionally difficult clients. It usually takes three to six years of practical, on-the-job experience in order to become a fully qualified interior designer or decorator.

As interior professionals gain experience, they can move into positions of greater responsibility and may eventually be promoted to such jobs as design department head or interior furnishings coordinator. Professionals who work with furnishings in architectural firms often become more involved in product design and sales. Designers and decorators can also establish their own businesses. Consulting is another common area of work for the established interior professional.

EARNINGS

Interior designers earned median annual salaries of $42,260 in 2006, according to the U.S. Department of Labor. The highest paid

10 percent earned more than $78,760, while the lowest paid 10 percent earned less than $24,270 annually. The U.S. Department of Labor reports the following mean salaries for interior designers by specialty: architectural and engineering services, $50,300; specialized design services, $50,190; and furniture stores, $43,330. In general, interior designers and decorators working in large urban areas make significantly more than those working in smaller cities.

Designers and decorators at interior design firms can earn a straight salary, a salary plus a bonus or commission, or a straight commission. Such firms sometimes pay their employees a percentage of the profits as well. Self-employed professionals may charge an hourly fee, a flat fee, or a combination of the two, depending on the project. Some designers and decorators charge a percentage based on the cost of materials bought for each project.

The benefits enjoyed by interior designers and decorators, like salaries and bonuses, depend on the particular employer. Benefits may include paid vacations, health and life insurance, paid sick or personal days, employee-sponsored retirement plans, and an employer-sponsored 401(k) program.

WORK ENVIRONMENT

Working conditions for interior designers and decorators vary, depending on where they are employed. While professionals usually have an office or a studio, they may spend the day at a department store, architectural firm, or construction site working with the decorating materials sold by the firm and the clients who have purchased them. In addition, designers often go on-site to consult with and supervise the projects being completed by various craftworkers.

Whether designers or decorators are employed by a firm or operate their own businesses, much of their time is spent in clients' homes and businesses. While more and more offices are using the services of interior designers and decorators, the larger part of the business still lies in the area of home design. Residential designers and decorators work intimately with customers, planning, selecting materials, receiving instructions, and sometimes subtly guiding the customers' tastes and choices in order to achieve an atmosphere that is both aesthetic and functional.

While designers and decorators employed by department stores, furniture stores, or design firms often work regular 40-hour weeks, self-employed professionals usually work irregular hours—including evenings and weekends—in order to accommodate their clients' schedules. Deadlines must be met, and if there have been problems and delays on the job, the designer or decorator must work hard to complete the project on schedule. In general, the more successful the individual becomes, the longer and more irregular the hours.

The interior professional's main objective is ultimately to please the customer and thus establish a good reputation. Customers may be difficult at times. They may often change their minds, forcing the designer or decorator to revise plans. Despite difficult clients, the work is interesting and provides a variety of activities.

OUTLOOK

Employment opportunities are expected to be good for interior designers and decorators through 2014, according to the U.S. Department of Labor. However, since the services of design professionals are in many ways a luxury, the job outlook is heavily dependent on the economy. In times of prosperity, there is a steady increase in jobs. When the economy slows down, however, opportunities in the field decrease markedly.

Marketing futurist Faith Popcorn predicts that people will be staying home more (cocooning) and that there will be an increase in what she calls "fantasy adventure." This trend is based on people's desire to stay at home but, at the same time, feel like they are in exotic, remote places. In the future, Popcorn sees homes containing rooms designed like Las Vegas-style resorts, African plains, and other interesting destinations. Both cocooning and fantasy adventure will further add to the many opportunities that will be available to interior designers.

According to the International Interior Design Association's Industry Advisory Council (IAC), a number of trends specific to the industry will also positively influence the employment outlook for interior designers and decorators. Clients in all market areas, for example, will develop an appreciation for the value of interior design work as well as increased respect for the interior professional's expertise. In addition, businesses, ever mindful of their employees' safety, health, and general welfare, will rely more heavily on designers to create interior atmospheres that will positively impact workplace performance.

The IAC also notes the importance of technology in the field of interior design. In addition to affecting the design of homes, technology will impact the production of design materials as well as create the need for multidisciplinary design. Professionals both familiar and comfortable with technology will definitely have an edge in an ever-competitive job market.

While competition for good designing and decorating positions is expected to be fierce, especially for those lacking experience, there is currently a great need for industrial interior designers in housing developments, offices, restaurants, hospital complexes, senior care facilities, hotels, and other large building projects. In addition, as construction of houses increases, there will be many projects available for residential designers and decorators. Designers with strong knowledge of ergonomics and green design will also enjoy excellent job prospects.

FOR MORE INFORMATION

For industry trends, career guidance, and other resources, contact
American Society of Interior Designers
608 Massachusetts Avenue, NE
Washington, DC 20002-6006
Tel: 202-546-3480
http://www.asid.org

For a list of accredited interior design programs, contact
Council for Interior Design Accreditation
146 Monroe Center, NW, Suite 1318
Grand Rapids, MI 49503-2822
Tel: 616-458-0400
Email: info@accredit-id.org
http://www.accredit-id.org

For information on continuing education, publications, and a list of accredited graduate programs in interior design, contact
Interior Design Educators Council
7150 Winton Drive, Suite 300
Indianapolis, IN 46268-4398
Tel: 317-328-4437
Email: info@idec.org
http://www.idec.org

For information on the industry, contact
International Interior Design Association
222 Merchandise Mart, Suite 1540
Chicago, IL 60654-1386
Tel: 888-799-4432
Email: iidahq@iida.org
http://www.iida.com

For information on accredited interior design programs, contact
National Association of Schools of Art and Design
11250 Roger Bacon Drive, Suite 21
Reston, VA 20190-5248

Tel: 703-437-0700
Email: info@arts-accredit.org
http://nasad.arts-accredit.org

For information on the Interior Design Experience Program, contact
National Council for Interior Design Qualification
1200 18th Street, NW, Suite 1001
Washington, DC 20036-2506
Tel: 202-721-0220
http://www.ncidq.org

For information on certification, contact
National Kitchen and Bath Association
687 Willow Grove Street
Hackettstown, NJ 07840-1713
Tel: 800-843-6522
http://www.nkba.org

For useful information about interior design, visit
Dezignare Interior Design Collective
http://dezignare.com

For useful career information, visit
Careers in Interior Design
http://www.careersininteriordesign.com

═══ **INTERVIEW** ═══

Susan Septer is the owner of Susan Septer Design, LLC in Victoria, Minnesota. She is a member of the American Society of Interior Designers and a certified kitchen designer through the National Kitchen and Bath Association, and has worked as an interior designer since 1973. (Visit http://www.septerdesign.com to learn more about her work.) Susan discussed her career with the editors of Careers in Focus: Art.

Q. Please tell us about your business.
A. I specialize in kitchens, bathrooms, and built-in areas within the home. The majority of my work is with clients who are remodeling an outdated home that no longer fits their lifestyle. I spend time getting to know my clients to find out what does and does not work in their existing kitchen so the design fits their lifestyle.

Q. Why did you decide to become an interior designer?

A. I am a visual person influenced by my surroundings. I enjoy analyzing how to improve the layout of a space and finding ways to make a room more user friendly. As a child I would construct rooms out of cardboard boxes so I guess it was an interest that developed early in my life.

Q. What do you like most and least about your job?

A. I enjoy working directly with homeowners to solve space-planning problems, to find a better solution for their kitchen layout, and help them to have a beautiful kitchen that they are excited to use. I least like the time it takes to go over the details of an order to be sure it is accurate, and I don't enjoy when things come up that are out of my control, but have an affect on my work.

Q. What advice would you give to high school students who are interested in becoming interior designers?

A. Take advantage of the various art classes to experience different mediums, think about how history has influenced furnishings and art throughout time when you are in an English or social studies class, and don't ignore the business aspects of design such as marketing and accounting.

Q. What is the future employment outlook in the field?

A. I believe demand will create many opportunities to design for the aging baby boomers so that they can live independently in an environment that matches the lifestyle they enjoy now. The demographics of our population will determine where the next opportunities will be.

Jewelers and Jewelry Repairers

OVERVIEW

Jewelers create, either from their own design or one by a design specialist, rings, necklaces, bracelets, and other jewelry out of gold, silver, or platinum. *Jewelry repairers* alter ring sizes, reset stones, and refashion old jewelry. Restringing beads and stones, resetting clasps and hinges, and mending breaks in ceramic and metal pieces also are aspects of jewelry repair. A few jewelers are also trained as *gemologists*, who examine, grade, and evaluate gems, or *gem cutters,* who cut, shape, and polish gemstones. Many jewelers also repair watches and clocks. There are about 42,000 jewelers employed in the United States.

HISTORY

People have always worn adornments of some type. Early cave dwellers fashioned jewelry out of shells or the bones, teeth, or claws of animals. Beads have been found in the graves of prehistoric peoples. During the Iron Age, jewelry was made of ivory, wood, or metal. Precious stones were bought and sold at least 4,000 years ago in ancient Babylon, and there was widespread trade in jewelry by the Phoenicians and others in the Mediterranean and Asia Minor. The ancient Greeks and Romans were particularly fond of gold. Excavations of ancient Egyptian civilization show extremely well-crafted jewelry. It is believed that during this time jewelers first combined gems with precious metals.

Many of the metals jewelers use today, such as gold, silver, copper, brass, and iron, were first discovered or used by ancient jewelers. During the Hashemite Empire, a court jeweler discovered iron while seeking a stronger metal to use in battles. During the Renaissance period in Europe, jewelers became increasingly skillful. Artists such as Botticelli and Cellini used gold and silver with precious stones of every sort to create masterpieces of the gold and silversmiths' trades. Jewelers perfected the art of enameling during this time.

Many skilled artisans brought their trades to Colonial America. The first jewelers were watchmakers, silversmiths, and coppersmiths. In early America, a versatile craft worker might create a ring or repair the copper handle on a cooking pot. By the 1890s, New York City had emerged as a center of the precious metal jewelry industry. It became a center for the diamond trade as well as for other precious stones. The first jewelry store, as we know it today, opened at the turn of the 19th century.

By the early 20th century, machines were used to create jewelry, and manufacturing plants began mass production of costume jewelry. These more affordable items quickly became popular and made jewelry available to large numbers of people.

New York City continues today as a leading center of the precious metals industry and jewelry manufacturing in the United States. Along with Paris and London, New York is a prime location for many fine jewelry designers.

During the 1980s, a small niche of jewelers began creating their own designs and either making them themselves or having other jewelers fabricate them. Also called *jewelry artists,* they differ from more traditional designers both in the designs they create and the methods and materials they use. They sell their designer lines of jewelry in small boutiques, galleries, or at crafts shows or market them to larger retail stores. Many of these jewelers open their own stores. The American Jewelry Design Council was founded in 1990 to help promote designer jewelry as an art form.

THE JOB

Jewelers may design, make, sell, or repair jewelry. Many jewelers combine two or more of these skills. Designers conceive and sketch ideas for jewelry that they may make themselves or have made by another craftsperson. The materials used by the jeweler and the jewelry repairer may be precious, semiprecious, or synthetic. They work with valuable stones such as diamonds and rubies, and precious metals such as gold, silver, and platinum. Some jewelers use synthetic stones in their jewelry to make items more affordable.

The jeweler begins by forming an item in wax or metal with carving tools. The jeweler then places the wax model in a casting ring and pours plaster into the ring to form a mold. The mold is inserted into a furnace to melt the wax and a metal model is cast from the plaster mold. The jeweler pours the precious molten metal into the mold or uses a centrifugal casting machine to cast the article. Cutting, filing, and polishing are final touches the jeweler makes to the piece.

Jewelers do most of their work sitting down. They use small hand and machine tools, such as drills, files, saws, soldering irons, and jewelers' lathes. They often wear an eye loupe, or magnifying glass. They constantly use their hands and eyes and need good finger and hand dexterity.

Most jewelers specialize in creating certain kinds of jewelry or focus on a particular operation, such as making, polishing, or stone-setting models and tools. Specialists include gem cutters; stone setters; fancy-wire drawers; locket, ring, and hand chain makers; and sample makers.

Silversmiths design, assemble, decorate, or repair silver articles. They may specialize in one or more areas of the jewelry field such as repairing, selling, or appraising. *Jewelry engravers* carve text or graphic decorations on jewelry. *Watchmakers* repair, clean, and adjust mechanisms of watches and clocks.

Gem and diamond workers select, cut, shape, polish, or drill gems and diamonds using measuring instruments, machines, or hand tools. Some work as diamond die polishers, while others are gem cutters.

Other jewelry workers perform such operations as precision casting and modeling of molds, or setting precious and semiprecious stones for jewelry. They may make gold or silver chains and cut designs or lines in jewelry using hand tools or cutting machines. Other jewelers work as pearl restorers or jewelry bench hands.

Assembly line methods are used to produce costume jewelry and some types of precious jewelry, but the models and tools needed for factory production must be made by highly skilled jewelers. Some molds and models for manufacturing are designed and created using computer-aided design/manufacturing systems. Costume jewelry often is made by a die stamping process. In general, the more precious the metals, the less automated the manufacturing process.

Some jewelers and jewelry repairers are self-employed; others work for manufacturing and retail establishments. Workers in a manufacturing plant include skilled, semiskilled, and unskilled positions. Skilled positions include jewelers, ring makers, engravers, toolmakers, electroplaters, and stonecutters and setters. Semiskilled positions include polishers, repairers, toolsetters, and solderers. Unskilled workers are press operators, carders, and linkers.

Although some jewelers operate their own retail stores, an increasing number of jewelry stores are owned or managed by individuals who are not jewelers. In such instances, the owner may employ a jeweler or jewelry repairer, or the store may send its repairs to a trade shop operated by a jeweler who specializes in repair work. Jewelers who operate their own stores sell jewelry, watches, and, frequently, merchandise such as silverware, china, and glassware. Many retail jewelry stores are located in or near large cities, with the eastern section of the country providing most of the employment in jewelry manufacturing.

Other jobs in the jewelry business include *appraisers,* who examine jewelry and determine its value and quality; *sales staff,* who set up and care for jewelry displays, take inventory, and help customers; and *buyers,* who purchase jewelry, gems, and watches from wholesalers and resell the items to the public in retail stores.

REQUIREMENTS

High School
A high school education usually is necessary for those desiring to enter the jewelry trade. While you are in high school, take courses in chemistry, physics, mechanical drawing, and art. Computer-aided design classes will be especially beneficial to you if you are planning to design jewelry. Sculpture and metalworking classes will prepare you for design and repair work.

Postsecondary Training
A large number of educational and training programs are available in jewelry and jewelry repair. Trade schools and community colleges offer a variety of programs, including classes in basic jewelry-making skills, techniques, use and care of tools and machines, stone setting, casting, polishing, and gem identification. Programs usually run from six months to one year, although individual classes are shorter and can be taken without enrolling in an entire program.

Some colleges and universities offer programs in jewelry store management, metalwork, and jewelry design. You can also find classes at fashion institutes, art schools, and art museums. In addition, you can take correspondence courses and continuing education classes. For sales and managerial positions in a retail store, college experience is usually helpful. Recommended classes are sales techniques, gemology, advertising, accounting, business administration, and computers.

The work of the jeweler and jewelry repairer may also be learned through an apprenticeship or by informal on-the-job training. The latter often includes instruction in design, quality of precious stones, and chemistry of metals. The apprentice becomes a jeweler upon the successful completion of a two-year apprenticeship and passing written and oral tests covering the trade. The apprenticeship generally focuses on casting, stone setting, and engraving.

Most jobs in manufacturing require on-the-job training, although many employers prefer to hire individuals who have completed a technical education program.

Certification or Licensing

Certification is available in several areas through the Jewelers of America, a trade organization. Those who do bench work (the hands-on work creating and repairing jewelry) can be certified at one of four levels: certified bench jeweler technician, certified bench jeweler, certified senior bench jeweler, and certified master bench jeweler. Each certification involves passing a written test and a bench test. Jewelers of America also offers certification for management and sales workers. Although voluntary, these certifications show that a professional has met certain standards for the field and is committed to this work.

Other Requirements

Jewelers and jewelry repairers need to have extreme patience and skill to handle the expensive materials of the trade. Although the physically disabled may find employment in this field, superior hand-eye coordination is essential. Basic mechanical skills such as filing, sawing, and drilling are vital to the jewelry repairer. Jewelers who work from their own designs need creative and artistic ability. They also should have a strong understanding of metals and their properties. Retail jewelers and those who operate or own trade shops and manufacturing establishments must work well with people and have a knowledge of merchandising and business management and practices. Sales staff should be knowledgeable and friendly, and buyers must have good judgment, self-confidence, and leadership abilities. Because of the expensive nature of jewelry, some people working in the retail industry are bonded, which means they must pass the requirements for an insurance company to underwrite them.

EXPLORING

If you are interested in becoming a jeweler or jewelry repairer, you can become involved in arts and crafts activities and take classes in crafts and jewelry making. Many community education programs are available through high schools, park districts, or local art stores and museums. Hobbies such as metalworking and sculpture are useful in becoming familiar with metals and the tools jewelers use. Visits to museums and fine jewelry stores to see collections of jewelry can be helpful.

If you are interested in the retail aspect of this field, you should try to find work in a retail jewelry store on a part-time basis or during the summer. A job in sales, or even as a clerk, can provide a firsthand introduction to the business. A retail job will help you become familiar with a jewelry store's operations, its customers, and the jewelry sold. In addition, you will learn the terminology unique to the jewelry field. Working in a store with an in-house jeweler or jewelry repairer provides many opportunities to observe and speak with a professional engaged in this trade. In a summer or part-time job as a bench worker or assembly line worker in a factory, you may perform only a few of the operations involved in making jewelry, but you will be exposed to many of the skills used within a manufacturing plant.

You also may want to visit retail stores and shops where jewelry is made and repaired or visit a jewelry factory. Some boutiques and galleries are owned and operated by jewelers who enjoy the opportunity to talk to people about their trade. Art fairs and craft shows where jewelers exhibit and sell their products provide a more relaxed environment where jewelers are likely to have time to discuss their work.

EMPLOYERS

Approximately 42,000 jewelers and precious stone and metal workers are employed in the United States. Jewelers work in a variety of settings, from production work in multinational corporations to jewelry stores and repair shops. Some jewelers specialize in gem and diamond work, watchmaking, jewelry appraisal, repair, or engraving, where they may work in manufacturing or at the retail level. Other jewelers work only as appraisers. In most cases, appraisals are done by store owners or jewelers who have years of experience. About 40 percent of all jewelers are self-employed. The majority of the self-employed jewelers own their own stores or repair shops or specialize in designing and creating custom jewelry. Top states for jewelry manufacturing include Rhode Island, New York, and California.

STARTING OUT

A summer or part-time job in a jewelry store or the jewelry department of a department store will help you learn about the business. Another way to enter this line of work is to contact jewelry manufacturing establishments in major production centers. A trainee can acquire the many skills needed in the jewelry trade. The number of trainees accepted in this manner, however, is relatively small. Students who have completed a training program improve their chances of finding work as an apprentice or trainee. Students may learn about available jobs and apprenticeships through the career services offices of training schools they attend, from local jewelers, or from the personnel offices of manufacturing plants.

Those desiring to establish their own retail businesses find it helpful to first obtain employment with an established jeweler or a manufacturing plant. Considerable financial investment is required to open a retail jewelry store, and jewelers in such establishments find it to their advantage to be able to do repair work on watches as well as the usual jeweler's work. Less financial investment is needed to open a trade shop. These shops generally tend to be more successful in or near areas with large populations where they can take advantage of the large volume of jewelry business. Both retail jewelry stores and trade shops are required to meet local and state business laws and regulations.

ADVANCEMENT

There are many opportunities for advancement in the jewelry field. Jewelers and jewelry repairers can go into business for themselves once they have mastered the skills of their trade. They may create their own designer lines of jewelry that they market and sell, or they can open a trade shop or retail store. Many self-employed jewelers gain immense satisfaction from the opportunity to specialize in one aspect of jewelry or to experiment with new methods and materials.

Workers in jewelry manufacturing have fewer opportunities for advancement than in other areas of jewelry because of the declining number of workers needed. Plant workers in semiskilled and unskilled positions can advance based on the speed and quality of their work and by perseverance. On-the-job training can provide opportunities for higher-skilled positions. Workers in manufacturing who show proficiency can advance to supervisory and management positions, or they may leave manufacturing and go to work in a retail shop or trade shop.

The most usual avenue of advancement is from employee in a factory, shop, or store to owner or manager of a trade shop or retail store. Sales is an excellent starting place for people who want to own their own store. Sales staff receive firsthand training in customer relations as well as knowledge of the different aspects of jewelry store merchandising. Sales staff may become gem experts who are qualified to manage a store, and managers may expand their territory from one store to managing several stores in a district or region. Top management in retail offers many interesting and rewarding positions to people who are knowledgeable, responsible, and ambitious. Buyers may advance by dealing exclusively with fine gems that are more expensive, and some buyers become *diamond merchants,* buying diamonds on the international market.

Jewelry designers' success depends not only on the skill with which they make jewelry but also on the ability to create new designs and keep in touch with current trends in the consumer market. Jewelry designers attend craft shows, trade shows, and jewelry exhibitions to see what others are making and to get ideas for new lines of jewelry.

EARNINGS

Jewelers and precious stone and metal workers had median annual earnings of $29,750 in 2006, according to the U.S. Department of Labor. Salaries ranged from less than $17,760 to more than $54,940. Most jewelers start out with a base salary. With experience, they can charge by the number of pieces completed. Jewelers who work in retail stores may earn a commission for each piece of jewelry sold, in addition to their base salary.

Most employers offer benefit packages that include paid holidays and vacations and health insurance. Retail stores may offer discounts on store purchases.

WORK ENVIRONMENT

Jewelers work in a variety of environments. Some self-employed jewelers design and create jewelry in their homes; others work in small studios or trade shops. Jewelers who create their own designer lines of jewelry may travel to retail stores and other sites to promote their merchandise. Many designers also attend trade shows and exhibitions to learn more about current trends. Some sell their jewelry at both indoor and outdoor art shows and craft fairs. These shows are held on weekends, evenings, or during the week. Many jewelry artists live and work near tourist areas or in art communities.

Workers in jewelry manufacturing plants usually work in clean, air-conditioned, and relatively quiet environments. Workers in departments such as polishing, electroplating, and lacquer spraying may be exposed to fumes from chemicals and solvents. Workers who do bench work sit at workstations. Other workers stand at an assembly line for many hours at a time. Many workers in a manufacturing plant perform only one or two types of operations so the work can become repetitious. Most employees in a manufacturing plant work 35-hour workweeks, with an occasional need for overtime.

Retail store owners, managers, jewelers, and sales staff work a variety of hours and shifts that include weekends, especially during the Christmas season, the busiest time of year. Buyers may work more than 40 hours a week because they must travel to see wholesalers. Work settings vary from small shops and boutiques to large department stores. Most jewelry stores are clean, quiet, pleasant, and attractive. However, most jewelry store employees spend many hours on their feet dealing with customers, and buyers travel a great deal.

OUTLOOK

Employment of jewelers is expected to decline through 2014, according to the *Occupational Outlook Handbook*. Despite this prediction, jewelers and jewelry repairers will continue to be needed to replace those workers who leave the workforce or move to new positions. Since jewelry sales are increasing at rates that exceed the number of new jewelers entering the profession, employers are finding it difficult to find skilled employees.

Consumers now are purchasing jewelry from mass marketers, discount stores, catalogs, television shopping shows, and the Internet as well as from traditional retail stores. This may result in store closings or limited hiring.

The number of workers in manufacturing plants is declining because of increased automation, but opportunities for skilled workers should remain fairly steady. Demand in retail is growing for people who are skilled in personnel, management, sales and promotion, advertising, floor and window display, and buying. Opportunities will be best for graduates of training programs for jewelers or gemologists.

FOR MORE INFORMATION

For answers to frequently asked questions about jewelry, visit the society's Web site
American Gem Society
8881 West Sahara Avenue
Las Vegas, NV 89117-5865
Tel: 866-805-6500
http://www.americangemsociety.org

For information on designer jewelry, contact
American Jewelry Design Council
760 Market Street, Suite 900
San Francisco, CA 94102-2304
http://www.ajdc.org

For an information packet with tuition prices, application procedures, and course descriptions, contact
Gemological Institute of America
The Robert Mouawad Campus
5345 Armada Drive
Carlsbad, CA 92008-4602
Tel: 800-421-7250, ext. 4001 (admissions)
Email: admissions@gia.edu
http://www.gia.edu

For certification information, a school directory, and a copy of
Careers in the Jewelry Industry, *contact*
Jewelers of America
52 Vanderbilt Avenue, 19th Floor
New York, NY 10017-3827
Tel: 800-223-0673
Email: info@jewelers.org
http://www.jewelers.org

For career and school information, contact
Manufacturing Jewelers and Suppliers of America
45 Royal Little Drive
Providence, RI 02904-1861
Tel: 800-444-6572
Email: info@mjsa.org
http://mjsa.polygon.net

Medical Illustrators and Photographers

OVERVIEW

Medical illustrators and photographers use graphics, drawings, and photographs to make medical concepts easier to understand. Medical illustrators provide illustrations of anatomical and biological structures and processes, as well as surgical and medical techniques and procedures. Medical photographers take photos that communicate complex medical or scientific information for use in textbooks, professional journals, and other teaching materials.

HISTORY

Images used to depict medical procedures and anatomical parts started out as illustrations. Illustration figured prominently in the ancient civilizations of Mesopotamia, Egypt, and later Greek and Roman civilizations. Drawings depicting biological, zoological, and medical knowledge have also been found among ancient Assyrian, Babylonian, Egyptian, and Chinese societies. Modern illustration began during the Renaissance of the 15th and 16th centuries, with the work of Leonardo da Vinci, Andreas Vesalius, and Michelangelo Buonarotti.

In 1625, Francesco Stelluti used the newly invented microscope to create a series of drawings of a honeybee that were magnified 10 times. The microscope became an important tool for illustrators seeking to represent details of biological and medical processes.

With the invention of the camera, photographs were soon preferred in the medical world for their accurate and realistic depictions. The first medical photography, called photomicrography, was shot through a microscope.

Over time, tools have been developed to aid illustrators and photographers in their work. Illustrators have made use of parallel bars, compasses, French curves, and T squares, but the development of computer technology has largely replaced these mechanical tools with computer-aided design software. For medical photographers, the growing sophistication of cameras has made it possible to accurately capture medical processes with complete clarity.

QUICK FACTS

(continues)

O*NET-SOC
27-1013.01 (illustrators)
27-4021.02 (photographers)

THE JOB

Medical illustrators work in a specialized area of technical illustration. These illustrators are concerned with representing human anatomy and processes, as well as other biological information. Their work is found in medical textbooks, magazines and journals, advertisements for medical products, instructional films and DVDs, television programs, exhibits, lectures and presentations, and computer-assisted learning programs. Some medical illustrators create three-dimensional physical models, such as anatomical teaching models, models used for teaching medical procedures, and also prosthetics.

The role of the medical illustrator is to aid in making medical and biological information, procedures, and techniques more understandable. They combine knowledge of biology and anatomy with strong artistic and graphic skills.

Medical illustrators generally work with physicians, surgeons, biologists, and other scientists. When detailing a surgical procedure, they may observe the surgeon during surgery and ask him or her for advice about which parts of an operation to illustrate. Medical illustrators draw parts of the body, such as the eye, the skeletal structure, or the structure of a cell, for books, encyclopedias, medical product brochures, and related literature. They may illustrate the work of researchers, depicting research on new organisms or drugs. They may also assist in developing sophisticated computer simulations that allow physicians in training to "perform" a surgical procedure entirely on a computer before they are skilled enough to operate on actual patients.

A medical illustrator may work in a wide range of medical and biological areas or specialize in a particular area, such as cellular structure, disease, or the heart. Much of their work is done with computers; however, they must still have strong skills in traditional drawing and drafting techniques.

Some medical illustrators work as freelancers and contract their services out to hospitals, medical centers, and other organizations that require the services of a medical illustrator. Jennifer Fairman is a certified medical illustrator who is the owner of Fairman Studios, LLC, a medical and scientific illustration business located in Waltham, Massachusetts. As an owner of a freelance practice, her responsibilities extend a bit beyond the drawing table. "A typical day," she explains, "may involve a meeting with a client to discuss a new project, or I may attend a conference call from my studio to discuss the progress of an existing project. I could be sitting in a library doing research, or I may be invited to attend and observe a surgical procedure, which I will sketch while in the operating room. I may be sitting at the drawing table sketching out an idea for a project, or sitting at my computer, rendering an illustration or animation. I may have paperwork to do, like my bookkeeping, or I may have sales calls to follow up on in order to continue to drum up new work."

Like illustrators, medical photographers can vary their style depending on the purpose of a photograph. They often take photos to document patients' conditions before and after surgery, for example. This task requires technical proficiency in photography, but does not call for innovative use of space or lighting in a shot. Photos taken for brochures or advertising materials, however, can be stylized and dramatic. In this case, medical photographers use lighting, camera angles, and design principles to create different effects in their photos.

REQUIREMENTS

High School
While in high school, make sure to develop your skills in the two areas you'll need the most: science and art. Classes in anatomy, chemistry, biology, and nutrition will be useful. Aside from taking illustration and/or photography courses, check out classes in visual design, if available. Most medical illustrators and photographers use computers in their artwork, so gain familiarity with digital cameras and computer art, design, and layout programs.

Advanced Degree Programs in
Medical Illustration

There are only five advanced degree programs in medical illustration in the United States and Canada that are accredited by the Commission on Accreditation of Allied Health Education Programs. They are:

The Medical College of Georgia
Department of Medical Illustration
1120 15th Street, CJ1101
Augusta, GA 30912-0300
Tel: 706-721-3266
Email: medart@mcg.edu
http://www.mcg.edu/medart

University of Illinois–Chicago
Department of Biomedical and Health Information Sciences
919 West Taylor Street, Room 250, AHSB, MC 530
Chicago, IL 60612-7249
Tel: 312-996-7337
http://www.ahs.uic.edu/bhis/programs/bvis.php

The Johns Hopkins University School of Medicine
Department of Art as Applied to Medicine
1830 East Monument Street, Suite 7000
Baltimore, MD 21205-2100
Tel: 410-955-3213
http://www.hopkinsmedicine.org/medart

The University of Texas–Southwestern Medical Center at Dallas
5323 Harry Hines Boulevard
Dallas, TX 75390-7208
Tel: 214-648-3111
http://www.utsouthwestern.edu/utsw/home/gradschool/
biocommunications

University of Toronto
Medical Sciences Building, Room 2356
One King's College Circle
Toronto, ON M5S 1A8 Canada
Tel: 416-978-2659
http://www.bmc.med.utoronto.ca/bmc

Postsecondary Training

Most medical illustrators first obtain a bachelor's degree in either art or biology. After completing their undergraduate degree, they are required to complete an advanced degree program in medical illustration accredited by the Commission on Accreditation of Allied Health Education Programs (CAAHEP). The programs, which last from two to three years, are offered by four U.S. schools and one Canadian institution (see sidebar). Programs usually include training in traditional illustration and design techniques, computer illustration, two- and three-dimensional animation, prosthetics, medical computer graphics, instructional design and technology, photography, motion media production, and pharmaceutical advertising. Course work will also include pharmacology, basic sciences including anatomy and physiology, pathology, histology, embryology, neuroanatomy, and surgical observation and/or participation.

Most medical illustrators are members of the Association of Medical Illustrators (AMI). The AMI works with the CAAHEP to establish accreditation and curriculum standards, offer certification in medical illustration, and provide other educational and support services to members and prospective members of this profession.

Medical photographers must finish an associate's or bachelor's degree program that emphasizes art and photography. Very few schools offer graduate programs in medical photography. Completing a postsecondary degree in a photography-related field and taking additional course work in science will prepare you for this career.

Certification or Licensing

The Association of Medical Illustrators offers the designation, certified medical illustrator. To be eligible, applicants must graduate from an accredited program or obtain at least five years' experience and complete a course in gross anatomy with hands-on dissection.

Medical illustrators and photographers need to continue their education and training while pursuing their careers. Licensing is not required in either field. While certification is not mandatory, you must keep up with the latest innovations in design techniques, computer software, photography equipment, and presentation technology, as well as technological advances in the fields for which you provide illustrations or photos.

Other Requirements

To be a successful medical illustrator or photographer, you should possess manual dexterity, have good eyesight and color vision, and enjoy working with detail. Self-employed (or freelance) medical illustrators and photographers need good business and marketing skills.

EXPLORING

You can explore an interest in this career by taking art and photography courses. Participation in science clubs and fairs is also a good idea. Artists can always improve their drawing skills by practicing on their own, either producing original artwork, or making sketches from scientific drawings that appear in textbooks and reference manuals. Visit the AMI or the BioCommunications Association (BCA) Web sites (listed at the end of this article) for galleries of award-winning images. You should also consider contacting a medical illustrator or photographer to arrange an information interview about his or her career.

EMPLOYERS

Both medical illustrators and photographers are employed at hospitals, medical centers, and schools and academic institutions. Laboratories, pharmaceutical companies, publishers of medical and scientific textbooks, and advertising agencies also employ illustrators and photographers.

STARTING OUT

Graduates of medical illustration programs should develop a portfolio of their work to show to prospective employers or clients. Most schools offer career counseling and job placement assistance to their graduates. Job ads and employment agencies are also potential sources for locating work. Likewise, aspiring medical photographers should assemble a professional portfolio of their best photos to show potential employers.

Jennifer Fairman feels that networking is the best way to enter the career of medical illustrator. "I would encourage," she recommends, "a new medical illustrator to get involved in such organizations as the Association of Medical Illustrators or the Guild of Natural Science Illustrators. These two organizations not only attract individuals with similar interests, but also foster the continuing education of those individuals. Because our field is such a small niche, it is easy to network and find out where there are jobs. I often receive referrals for my business from my colleagues in these organizations."

Medical illustrators and photographers can also find job placement assistance with the AMI and BCA. Beginning illustrators and photographers should consider joining one of these professional associations not only for job leads, but also to meet other workers in the field and stay on top of trends and advancements in the industry.

ADVANCEMENT

After an illustrator or photographer gains experience, he or she will be given more challenging and unusual work. Those with strong computer skills will have the best chances for advancement. Illustrators and photographers can advance by developing skills in a specialized area, or even starting their own business.

Individuals who work for large hospitals or teaching institutions can become managers of media and communications departments. They can also go into teaching in colleges and universities at the undergraduate and graduate levels.

EARNINGS

According to the AMI, medical illustrators who have graduated from accredited graduate programs receive starting salaries that range from $40,000 to $45,000 per year. The average pay for an experienced medical illustrator ranges from $45,000 to $75,000 per year, depending on location and level of experience. At the high end, medical illustrators can earn $100,000 to $200,000 per year, particularly if they combine freelance work with a full-time position.

Medical photographers generally earn salaries similar to medical illustrators at the entry level. The field's competitiveness, though, sometimes leads to lower salaries for experienced photographers— around $35,000 to $40,000—than for experienced illustrators.

Medical illustrators and photographers employed by hospitals and other large institutions generally receive good benefits, including health and life insurance, pension plans, and vacation, sick, and holiday pay.

WORK ENVIRONMENT

Medical illustrators generally work in clean, well-lit offices. They spend a great deal of time at their desks, whether in front of a computer or at the drafting table. They are sometimes required to visit operating rooms and other medical settings.

Photographers, especially those employed by a large hospital, may have to run around during their day. They may be asked to take photos of a complicated surgery in the morning, and then shoot pictures at an official hospital event that night. They also may spend time in a darkroom or in front of a computer, looking for and preparing photos for publishing.

OUTLOOK

The outlook for employment as a medical illustrator is good. Because there are only a few graduate programs in medical illustration with small graduation classes, medical illustrators will find great demand for their skills. The field of medicine and science in general is always growing, and medical illustrators will be needed to depict new techniques, procedures, and discoveries.

Jennifer Fairman also sees excellent employment opportunities in medical illustration. "Medical illustrators," she says, "have gone from using traditional carbon pencil and pen and ink to the airbrush, and then the computer became a new instrument on our drawing tables. Now 2-D animation, 3-D modeling and animation, and the World Wide Web have opened new doors to growth and potential in the field of biocommunications. I see this trend continuing, allowing the field to expand and our visual messages to be carried even further, and for illustrators to become more specialized within different niche disciplines."

The demand for medical photographers has declined somewhat in recent years. Cost-cutting measures at institutions have led to increased purchases of stock photography rather than hiring photographers to take original photos. Some physicians also take their own photos, or rely on media members to take them. Despite slower growth, the constantly developing field of scientific information will ensure a continued need for medical photographers.

FOR MORE INFORMATION

For information on educational and career opportunities and certification for medical illustrators, contact
Association of Medical Illustrators
810 East 10th Street
Lawrence, KS 66044-3018
Tel: 866-393-4264
Email: hq@ami.org
http://medical-illustrators.org

For information on membership, contact
BioCommunications Association
220 Southwind Lane
Hillsborough, NC 27278-7907
Tel: 919-245-0906
Email: office@bca.org
http://www.bca.org

For information on membership, contact
Guild of Natural Science Illustrators
PO Box 652
Ben Franklin Station
Washington, DC 20044-0652
Tel: 301-309-1514
Email: gnsihome@his.com
http://www.gnsi.org

For membership information, contact
Health and Science Communications Association
39 Wedgewood Drive, Suite A
Jewett City, CT 06351-2420
Tel: 860-376-5915
http://www.hesca.org

For information on accredited art programs, contact
National Association of Schools of Art and Design
11250 Roger Bacon Drive, Suite 21
Reston, VA 20190-5248
Tel: 703-437-0700
Email: info@arts-accredit.org
http://nasad.arts-accredit.org

For information on the career of illustrator, contact
Society of Illustrators
128 East 63rd Street
New York, NY 10021-7303
Tel: 212-838-2560
Email: info@societyillustrators.org
http://www.societyillustrators.org

Multimedia Artists

OVERVIEW

Multimedia artists create art for commercial and fine art purposes by combining traditional artistic skills with new technologies such as computers, scanners, and digital cameras. Multimedia artists are innovators and are not bound by tradition or convention. They respond to cultural and societal stimuli and incorporate them into works of art.

HISTORY

Artists have incorporated technology into their artwork for more than 50 years, but multimedia art as it is known today can be traced back to the past few decades when new technologies such as computers, scanners, and digital cameras became available on a mass scale. Today, multimedia artists are constantly experimenting with the latest technologies to create innovative, challenging, and often beautiful works of fine and commercial art.

THE JOB

Multimedia artists use new technologies to create art for commercial and fine art purposes. Instead of a traditional paintbrush and canvas, they use a mouse, keyboard, scanner, digital camera, and other computer equipment to create their works. Their creations can be seen in both museum galleries or on commercial products. They may work as freelance artists, or work in computer and video gaming, advertising, animation, and other diverse industries.

Multimedia artists use their creative abilities and technological skills to produce original works of art to express ideas; to provide social and cultural commentary; to communicate messages; to sell

QUICK FACTS

School Subjects
Art
Computer science

Personal Skills
Artistic
Communication/ideas

Work Environment
Primarily indoors
Primarily one location

Minimum Education Level
Some postsecondary training

Salary Range
$30,390 to $51,350 to $92,720+

Certification or Licensing
None available

Outlook
About as fast as the average

DOT
N/A

GOE
N/A

NOC
5241

O*NET-SOC
27-1014.00

products; to explore color, texture, line, and other visual elements; and for many other purposes.

Many multimedia artists work as self-employed fine artists. They spend years developing their own style, focusing on a chosen subject, and refining their skills with their equipment. Most artists change styles subtly as they gain experience in their art and in their lives, and some experiment with different technology. For example, a multimedia artist may start out using digital photography to create realistic looking images, but might become more experimental over time, manipulating his or her images more for visual effect.

Multimedia fine artists spend a good deal of their time trying to sell their work, searching for appropriate galleries or art shows that fit their work and have good enough customer traffic to increase chances for a sale. The gallery owner and artist set the prices for pieces of art, and the gallery owner receives a commission on any work that sells. The relationship between the gallery owner and artists is often one of close cooperation. For example, a gallery owner may encourage artists to explore new techniques, styles, and ideas while helping to establish their reputation. As a multimedia artist becomes well-known, selling his or her work often becomes easier, and many well-known artists receive commissions for their art.

REQUIREMENTS

High School
In high school, take as many art courses as you can. While you will be specializing in computer- and technology-based art, all multimedia artists should have a good foundation in the traditional art disciplines, such as painting, illustration, ceramics, and photography. If your school has computer design or imaging classes, be sure to take those. These classes will give you experience in working with page layout programs and art/photo manipulation programs. General computing classes will be useful to help you get comfortable with using a computer and different software.

Outside of class, try working on the school newspaper or yearbook staff. This can provide valuable design experience. You could also volunteer to design flyers or posters for school events such as athletic tournaments or plays.

Postsecondary Training
There are no formal educational requirements for becoming a multimedia artist. Some people start out seeking an associate's degree in art before moving into the job market, while others start creat-

ing artwork on their own. Others pursue a four-year bachelor's of art degree at an art school, general college, or university. Some pursue degrees in computer science, graphic design, or other related field.

Typical classes taken by a multimedia art student include traditional studio art, computer graphics, digital imaging, digital photography, Web design, animation, and digital page layout.

Certification and Licensing

There is no traditional certification or licensing available for multimedia artists. Artists who sell their work to the public may have to obtain special permits from their local or state tax office. Artists should also check with the Internal Revenue Service to learn more about tax information related to income received from the sale of artwork.

Other Requirements

Like all artists, multimedia artists need creativity, imagination, patience, persistence, determination, independence, and sensitivity. However, unlike other artists, they also need excellent computer skills to be able to work with their high-tech tools and canvases. They need working knowledge of several of the common drawing, image editing, and page layout programs, such as Adobe Photoshop or Illustrator. Multimedia art can be created with both Macintosh systems and on PCs; in fact, many artists have both types of computers in their studios.

If your interest is in fine art, be prepared to take a second job, especially when you are starting out. With the proper training and educational background, many fine artists are able to work in art-related positions, such as art teachers, art directors, or graphic designers, while pursuing their art activities independently.

EXPLORING

There are countless ways to learn about art while you are in high school. Visit art museums and galleries to view as much art as you can. Experiment with all genres of art to expand your artistic horizons. Take art classes in school or at local community centers. Talk to your high school art teacher about the field, and see if he or she can help arrange an interview with a multimedia artist. Visit the Web sites of colleges and universities that offer training in multimedia art. Read about typical classes, the backgrounds of instructors, and other topics. You might even consider contacting a multimedia art professor with questions about the career.

EMPLOYERS

The majority of multimedia artists are employed on a freelance basis and exhibit or sell their work on their own. Some work for graphic design firms, publishing houses, advertising agencies, or other businesses.

STARTING OUT

The first and foremost step for a freelance multimedia artist is to develop a portfolio, or a collection of work. The portfolio, which should be carefully organized to showcase a wide variety of the artist's talent and capabilities, is an essential tool when looking for work. Artists just starting out build their portfolio using works created during school, internships, and volunteer positions, and then gradually add to it as they gain more on-the-job experience.

Local fairs and art shows often provide opportunities for new artists to display their work. Art councils are a good source of information on upcoming fairs. However, most successful artists are represented by a gallery or agent that displays their work and approaches potential buyers when new works are available. The gallery or agent gets a commission for each piece of artwork sold. Relationships between artists and gallery operators can occasionally be tricky, but such relationships can also be beneficial to both creator and seller. A good gallery operator encourages, supports, and believes in the artists he or she represents.

Many art schools and universities have career services offices to help graduates find jobs. Although multimedia artists are generally self-employed, many need to work at another job, at least initially, to support themselves while they establish a reputation.

Some multimedia artists are hired by graphic design firms, advertising agencies, publishing houses, or other businesses. These professionals must also have a strong portfolio. Potential employers rely on portfolios to evaluate talent and how that talent might be used to fit the company's needs.

ADVANCEMENT

Self-employed artists advance by becoming increasingly well-known for their work, which allows them to show their art at more prestigious galleries and perhaps command higher prices for their work. Multimedia artists with good business skills may open galleries to display their own and others' work. Those with the appropriate educational backgrounds may become art teachers, gallery directors, agents, writers, or critics.

Commercial multimedia artists can start out in publishing or advertising as graphic designers and with experience become art directors or account executives. Experienced multimedia artists, especially those with leadership capabilities, may be promoted to chief designer or move into other computer-related positions such as graphics programming, animation, or video/computer game design.

EARNINGS

The amount of money earned by multimedia artists varies greatly depending on the industry in which they work. Freelance artists set their own prices depending on the demand for the work. The price they charge is up to them, but much depends on the value the public places on their work. A particular item may sell for a few dollars or tens of thousands of dollars, or at any price in between. The price may increase considerably after it has been sold if the artist's work becomes well-known and in demand. According to the U.S. Department of Labor, the median annual earnings of salaried multimedia artists were $51,350 in 2006. Salaries ranged from less than $30,390 to more than $92,720. Freelance artists often earn little, especially when they are first starting out.

WORK ENVIRONMENT

Multimedia artists work primarily indoors and at one location. They work with pens, pencils, and paper as well as with scanners, computers, and other high-tech equipment.

The environment for multimedia artists employed by graphic design firms, publishing houses, advertising agencies, and other businesses is usually casual—business suits are not required—but busy and often fast paced.

OUTLOOK

Employment for visual artists, including multimedia artists, is expected to grow as fast as the average for all occupations through 2014, according to the U.S. Department of Labor. Whether working as freelance or commercial artists, multimedia artists should enjoy good employment prospects in coming years as more and more people turn to digital processes as a means to communicate and make an artistic expression.

FOR MORE INFORMATION

This organization helps artists market and sell their art. It offers marketing tools, a newsletter, a directory of artists, and reference resources.
ArtNetwork
PO Box 1360
Nevada City, CA 95959-1360
Tel: 530-470-0862
Email: info@artmarketing.com
http://www.artmarketing.com

Contact the NASAD for information on accredited arts programs.
National Association of Schools of Art and Design (NASAD)
11250 Roger Bacon Drive, Suite 21
Reston, VA 20190-5248
Tel: 703-437-0700
Email: info@arts-accredit.org
http://nasad.arts-accredit.org

The NEA was established by Congress in 1965 to support excellence in the arts. It offers grants to artists and arts organizations, as well as various community-based programs. Visit its Web site for more information.
National Endowment for the Arts (NEA)
1100 Pennsylvania Avenue, NW
Washington, DC 20506-0001
Tel: 202-682-5400
Email: webmgr@arts.endow.gov
http://arts.endow.gov

Museum Directors and Curators

OVERVIEW

A *museum director* is equivalent to the chief executive officer of a corporation. The museum director is responsible for the daily operations of the museum, for long-term planning, policies, any research conducted within the museum, and for the museum's fiscal health. Directors must also represent the museum at meetings with other museums, business and civic communities, and the museum's governing body. Finally, directors ensure that museums adhere to state and federal guidelines for safety in the workplace and hiring practices, as well as industry recommendations concerning the acquisitions and care of objects within the museum.

Museum curators care for objects in a museum's collection. The primary curatorial activities are maintenance, preservation, archiving, cataloging, study, and display of collection components. Curators must fund-raise to support staff in the physical care and study of collections. They also add to or alter a museum's collection by trading objects with other museums or purchasing new pieces. They educate others through scholarly articles and public programs that showcase the items.

HISTORY

More than any other museum workers, curators and directors are closely identified with the image and purposes of a museum, and the history of these positions has followed the fortunes of museums themselves.

QUICK FACTS

School Subjects
Art
Business
History

Personal Skills
Communication/ideas
Leadership/management

Work Environment
Primarily indoors
One location with some
  travel

Minimum Education Level
Bachelor's degree

Salary Range
$65,000 to $110,000 to
  $500,000+ (directors)
$24,000 to $46,300 to
  $152,000 (curators)

Certification or Licensing
None available

Outlook
About as fast as the average

DOT
102

GOE
12.03.04NOC
0511 (directors)
0512 (curators)

O*NET-SOC
25-4012.00

Early precolonial and colonial museums were privately owned "cabinets of curios," but occasionally they were attached to a library or philosophical society, which allowed restricted viewing to members only. As the cabinet evolved into the museum through organized collecting and increased public access, there simultaneously arose some confusion over the mission of a museum and how that mission might best be achieved. The goals of museums, even of the same museum over time, began to alternate between a professional concentration on acquiring and studying collections, with some indifference to the interests of the public, and a contrary focus on visitor education and entertainment that occasionally turned into spectacles and sideshows as museums sought to raise money by any means. According to Joel Orosz, museum historian and author of *Curators and Culture: The Museum Movement in America, 1740–1870* (University of Alabama Press, 2002), the alternating between museum professionalism and public education marked the first long span of U.S. museum history, from about 1740 to 1870. By 1870, however, the two trends had blended together, which Orosz refers to as the American compromise: both popular education and scholarly research would be held as equal, coexisting goals. This achievement, the author asserts, arose out of uniquely American conditions, prior to several decades of efforts by British and European museums to instate a similar mixture of goals, and permanently shaped the rest of U.S. museum history.

Orosz's analysis divides early museum history into roughly 20-year periods, during which either professionalism or popular education was influential. With few exceptions, curators and museum directors were unable to find a neutral middle ground. In the early 1800s, with the rise of a middle class, the museum world assessed its purpose. As old supporters of the professional museums retired, new leaders began to associate their museums with public libraries and schools. Lecture series, pamphlets, and collection-based education became standard parts of a museum's program of activities. Museums emphasized popular, self-education between 1820 and 1840 and have continued to include this feature in their missions since that time.

At different times during the first century of U.S. museum history, professionalism spurted ahead, driven by new scientific inventions and technologies, for most museums of the era were natural history museums. Popular education, on the other hand, benefited from improved mass transportation. Robert Fulton's design of the steamboat, the opening of the Erie Canal in 1825, and the rise of the railroads gave travelers an alternative to tiring and dusty journeys by horse-drawn coach and allowed people from states as far away as Ohio and Kentucky to include eastern seaboard museums in their occasional travel plans. As distant travelers sought out museums, curators were gratified and responded with programs of more general, less scholarly interest. The concept of a national museum, free to all and representative of the nation as a whole, took root in the popular imagination and was finally achieved in 1846 with the opening of the Smithsonian Institution.

Following a period of national economic prosperity and intense museum-building activities in the years 1950 to 1980, the American compromise has again reached center stage, this time in a controversial light. With less discretionary money flowing through the economy, some museum directors believe it is no longer economically viable to maintain what amounts to two separate enterprises under one roof. Because public service is at the forefront of a modern museum's mission, museums are focusing on exhibits and programs for the public at the expense of support for research. Few taxpayers are repeat visitors to museums in any one year, and even fewer have any notion of what it is that museum directors and curators do. The coming decade will likely see increased revenue-generating activities for museums, a temporary freeze on museum allocations for research areas, or both. The financial stress is not uniquely felt by museums, for other civic institutions, notably symphony orchestras, have folded or sharply curtailed programs in the past few years. The American compromise faces some restructuring, introducing a period of uncertainty for many museum employees.

THE JOB

A museum director's most important duties are administrative, including staff leadership, promoting fund-raising campaigns, and ensuring that the museum's mission is carried out. Directors of large museums may have the assistance of several divisional directors with the authority for specific areas of museum management, such as a director of finance, director of development, director of public programs, director of research, director of education, director of operations, and director of marketing and public relations. In recognition of the museum director's role as "director of directors," the museum director sometimes has the title of *executive director.*

One unusual but not uncommon activity for a museum director is the design of new facilities. A director may spend a year or more working with architects and planners to reconfigure existing areas of the museum, add a wing (to house a new collection of contemporary art, for example), or build a museum from the ground up. Construction can be expected to draw resources away from other museum operations and may be accompanied by a massive capital campaign.

Every museum is unique in its mission, the community it serves, its resources, and the way it operates. The responsibilities of directors, therefore, vary widely. Directors of children's art museums typically have a background in education and apply educational philosophies to the design of exhibits and programs suitable for children. Interactive displays, live interpretation, and hands-on art studios are frequent components of children's museums, and community outreach programs help ensure that children of all backgrounds benefit from the museum's programs.

Directors of art museums typically have academic credentials in a specific art historical field and good financial and fund-raising skills to manage costly collections. The director may be personally involved in making acquisitions for the museum. Directors of museums reflecting a specific culture, such as Mexican, Asian, or Native American culture, need knowledge of that culture and diplomatic skills to arrange the exchange of exhibit material. An issue facing art museums today is the opinion that such institutions are for well-to-do patrons. Art museums are countering that impression by developing programs of interest to people from less advantaged backgrounds.

A curator's chief responsibilities include study and preservation of the museum's collections. Depending on the museum's size, resources, and deployment of staff, those responsibilities may be expressed in several different directions. In museums with a large curatorial staff, *senior curators* may function primarily as administrators, overseeing departmental budgets and hiring new curators. In a different employment environment, curators may focus closely on the study and shape of the collections, exchanging materials with other museums or acquiring new works of art or the correspondence of an artist to create a representative study collection of importance to scholarly work. In a third type of environment, curators may be primarily educators who describe and present collections to the visiting public. At any time, museum administrators may ask curators to redirect efforts toward a different goal of priority to the museum. Thus, a curator develops or brings to the position substantial knowledge of the materials in the collection, and that knowledge is used by the museum for a changing mix of purposes over time.

Curators may also spend time in the field or as visiting scholars at other museums as a means of continuing research related to the home institution's collections. Fieldwork is usually supported by grants from external sources. As specialists in their disciplines, curators may teach classes in local schools and universities, sometimes serving as academic advisors to doctoral degree candidates whose research is based on museum holdings. Almost all curators supervise a staff ranging from volunteers, interns, and students to research associates, collections managers, technicians, junior curators, and secretarial staff. Some sort of written work, whether it is labeling exhibits, preparing brochures for museum visitors, or publishing in scholarly journals, is typically part of the position.

In related positions, *collections managers* and *curatorial assistants* perform many of the same functions as curators, with more emphasis on study and cataloging of the collections and less involvement with administration and staff supervision. The educational requirements for these positions may be the same as for a curatorial position. A curatorial candidate may accept a position as collections manager while awaiting a vacancy on the curatorial staff, since the opportunity to study, publish research, and conduct fieldwork is usually equally available in both positions. In art, historical, and anthropological museums, *registrars* and *archivists* may act as collections managers by cataloging and preserving documents and objects and making information on these items available for scholarly use.

Once hired, curators embark on what is essentially a lifelong program of continuing self-education in museum practices. Curators of large collections must remain current with preservation techniques, including climate control and pest control methods. The human working environment can affect collections in unpredictable ways. As an example, high humidity may degrade the preservation environment of a collection of Renaissance-era wood panel paintings, which may mean that humidity monitoring equipment and climate-control technology will need to be installed to ensure that the collection does not deteriorate.

An important development in collections management is computerized cataloging of holdings for registry in national electronic databases. A number of larger museums and universities are working together to standardize data entry fields for these electronic registries, after which data on every item in a collection must be entered by hand and cross-checked for accuracy. Concurrently, there is a trend toward publishing through nonprint media, such as academic networks administered by the National Science Foundation. Continuing self-education in electronic technologies and participation in national conferences addressing these issues will be expected of curators throughout the upcoming decade and beyond, for electronic storage and retrieval systems have radically changed the face of collections management.

REQUIREMENTS

High School

Museum directors and curators need diverse educational backgrounds to perform well in their jobs. At the high school level, you should take courses in English, literature, creative writing, history, art, the sciences, speech, business, and foreign language. These courses will give you the general background knowledge needed to understand both the educational and administrative functions of museums. Math and computer skills are also essential. Museum directors and curators are responsible for preparing budgets and seeking funds from corporations and federal agencies.

Postsecondary Training

Museum directors and curators must have at least a bachelor's degree. Some colleges and universities offer undergraduate degrees in museology, or the study of museums. Most museums require their directorial staff and chief curators to hold doctoral degrees. Directors and curators usually work in museums that specialize in art, history, or science. These individuals often have degrees in fields related to the museum's specialty. Directors often have advanced degrees in business management, public relations, or marketing. All curators must have a good working knowledge of the art, objects, and cultures represented in their collections.

Other Requirements

Excellent written and oral communication skills are essential. Directors have a primary responsibility to supervise museum staff members, relay information to museum board members, and acquire funding for all museum programming. Museum directors must have extraordinary people skills and feel at ease when soliciting funds. Curators must have excellent research skills. They must be able to meet deadlines, write scholarly articles, and give presentations while managing their traditional museum duties. Museum directors and curators should be well organized and flexible.

Occasionally museums have specific requirements, such as foreign language fluency for an art or anthropology museum or practical computer skills for a science or natural history museum. These skills are ordinarily acquired as part of the background study within the student's area of concentration and do not pose special problems.

EXPLORING

Because of the diversity of U.S. museums and the academic background required for directorship and curatorial positions, high school students should simply concentrate on doing well in academic studies as preparation for either field. Museum directorships and curatorial positions are highly competitive and reward high academic achievement. Outside of school, participation in clubs that involve fund-raising activities can serve as a strong introduction to one important aspect of a museum director's job. Becoming the

Did You Know?

- Museums in the United States receive more than 600 million visits each year.
- Art museums are the fourth most popular type of museum in the United States (by number of visits).
- Seventy-three percent of museums are private, nonprofit institutions.
- More than one-third of museums do not charge an admission fee. The median admission fee for museums that do charge admission is $6.

Source: *2006 Museum Financial Information*, American Association of Museums

president of one of these clubs can provide you with supervisory skills and experience with delegating authority.

Museums offer public programs for people of all ages. Field trips or tours introduce students to activities conducted by local museums. College-age students may work at museums as volunteers or perhaps as interns for course credit. Depending on the museum's needs, volunteers and interns may be placed anywhere in the museum, including administration, archives, and other areas where a student may observe staff functions firsthand.

EMPLOYERS

Museums as well as historical societies and state and federal agencies with public archives and libraries hire directors and curators. These institutions are located throughout the world, in both small and large cities, and are responsible for providing public access to their collections. Museums and similar institutions employ directors and curators to fulfill their educational goals through continued research, care of collections, and public programs.

STARTING OUT

Museology, or the study of museums, is offered as an undergraduate major by some colleges in the United States, but most museum workers at all levels enter museum work because they possess specific skills and a body of knowledge useful to a particular museum. For a museum director, as for a well-qualified curator, this translates into content knowledge, managerial and administrative skills,

fund-raising ability, leadership ability, and excellent communication skills for effective interaction with the media and the board
of trustees. While the role of a curator is focused primarily on
collections and the role of director is often more administrative
and interpersonal, the two positions both require a great degree of
knowledge across the board regarding the museum's mission statement, acquisitions, and community involvement.

Museum directors typically move into a directorship in one
of three ways: laterally, from a previous directorship of another
museum; vertically, from an administrative or curatorial position
within the same museum; or laterally from a different sphere of
employment, such as a university presidency, business management,
government agency, or law practice.

A position as curator usually is not anticipated and prepared for
in advance, but becomes available as an employment option following a long period of training in a discipline. College and advanced
degree students who have identified a curatorial position as a career
goal may be able to apply for curatorial internships of varying terms,
usually a year or less. Interns typically work on a project identified
by the museum, which may involve only one task or several different tasks. Additionally, museums thrive on a large base of volunteer
labor, and this method of gaining museum experience should not
be overlooked. Curators may ask volunteers to assist in a variety of
tasks, ranging from clerical duties to conservation and computerized cataloging. When funds are available, volunteer work may be
converted to hourly paid work.

ADVANCEMENT

Museum directors typically succeed one another, moving from
smaller museums to larger museums or from a general to a specialty
museum. A museum directorship is a lifetime career goal and may
be held for decades by the same person. A museum director who
retires from the position is well prepared to sit on state or national
advisory councils to the arts and sciences. Some return to academic
life through teaching, research, or curricula development. Others
provide oversight and guidance to large institutions, sit on corporate
boards, or become involved in the start-up of new museums.

Curatorial positions follow the assistant, associate, and full (or
senior) track of academic employment, with advancement depending
on research and publishing, education, and service to the institution.
A curator with a taste for and skill in administration may serve as
departmental chair or may seek a higher administrative post.

In the course of their museum duties, curators may act as advisors to or principals in external nonprofit endeavors, such as providing technical assistance and labor to aid a developing country in the study of its artistic history or archaeological past. Many teach in local schools or universities. Curators who leave museum work may devote themselves full time to these or similar pursuits, although a university professorship as a second choice is difficult to achieve, for curators and professors are essentially competing for the same market position and have similar credentials. Occasionally, curators find fieldwork so compelling that they leave not only the museum, but also all formal employment, relying on grants and personal contributions from supporters to fund their work. To maintain an independent life as a researcher without formal affiliation requires a high profile in the discipline, continuing demonstration of productivity in the form of new research and publications, and some skill in self-promotion.

EARNINGS

The salaries of museum directors and curators cover a broad range, reflecting the diversity, size, and budget of U.S. museums, along with the director or curator's academic and professional achievements. In general, museum workers' salaries are low compared to salaries for similar positions in the business world or in academia. This is due in part to the large number of people competing for the relatively small number of positions available. At the high end of the scale, museum directors at museums like the Whitney Museum of American Art and the Metropolitan Museum of Art in New York City, or the Art Institute of Chicago earn more than $500,000 a year.

A survey of its members conducted by the Association of Art Museum Directors reported that the average salary of an art museum director is roughly $110,000. The average salary of a deputy director ranges from $65,000 to $123,000, while the average salary of an assistant to the director is roughly $31,000. The same study reported entry-level curatorial positions, often titled curatorial assistant or curatorial intern, as averaging $24,000, while assistant curator salaries average from $26,000 to $37,000 per year. Both the position of associate curator, a title with supervisory duties, and the position of curator of exhibitions average $34,000 to $53,000. Chief curator salaries average $57,000, but, as with many museum titles, may be considerably higher or lower depending on the demands of the job and the museum's overall budget. Curators directing an ongoing program of conservation and acquisitions in a large, national or international urban museum command the highest salaries and may earn as much as $152,000.

According to the U.S. Department of Labor, the median annual earnings of curators were $46,300 in 2006. Salaries ranged from less than $26,320 to more than $80,030. Museum curators employed by the federal government in nonsupervisory, supervisory, and managerial positions had mean annual earnings of $68,230 in 2006.

Fringe benefits, including paid vacations and sick leave, medical and dental insurance, and retirement plans, vary between museum directors and curators and according to each employing institution's policies.

WORK ENVIRONMENT

The directorship of a museum is an all-consuming occupation. Considerable travel, program development, fund-raising, and staff management may be involved. Evenings and weekends are often taken up by social activities involving museum donors or affiliates. A museum director must be willing to accept the pressure of answering to the museum's board of trustees while also overseeing museum staff and handling public relations.

As new issues affecting museums arise in the national consciousness and draw media attention, a director must be able to respond appropriately. A delicate balance must be maintained between the role of a museum as a civic institution, as reflected in the kinds of programs and exhibits developed for the public, and the less visible but equally important role of the museum as manager of the objects in its care, as reflected in conservation, research, publishing efforts, and the availability of the collections to visiting scholars. Museum directors must juggle competing interests and requests for the museum's resources.

The office of a director is typically housed within the museum. Many directors have considerable staff support, to which they can delegate specific areas of responsibility, and thus must have strong interpersonal and diplomatic skills.

Curators typically have an office in a private area of the museum, but may have to share office space. Employment conditions and benefits are more like those of industry than academia, although the employment contract may stipulate that the curator is free to pursue a personal schedule of fieldwork for several weeks during the year.

A curatorial post and a directorship are typically 9-to-5 jobs, but that does not take into account the long hours of study necessary to sustain scholarly research, weekend time spent on public programs, or evening meetings with donors, trustees, and museum affiliates. The actual hours spent on curatorial-related and directorship activities may be double those of the employment contract. Directors and curators must enjoy their work, be interested in museum operations and a museum's profile in the community, and willingly put in the necessary time. Becoming a museum director only occurs after years of dedication to the field and a great deal of tenacity. Likewise, curatorial positions are won by highly educated, versatile people, who in turn accept long hours and relatively (in comparison to other industries) low pay in exchange for doing work they love.

OUTLOOK

There are few openings for directors and curators and competition for them is high. New graduates may have to start as interns, volunteers, assistants, or research associates before finding full-time curator or director positions. Turnover is very low in museum work, so museum workers may have to stay in a lower-level position for some years before advancing to a director or curator position. Employment for museum directors and curators is expected to increase about as fast as the average for all occupations through 2014, according to the *Occupational Outlook Handbook*. The best opportunities are in art and history museums.

Curators must be able to develop revenue-generating public programs based on the study collections and integrate themselves firmly into programs of joint research with area institutions (other museums or universities) or national institutions, ideally programs of some duration and supported by external funding. Museums are affected by economic conditions and the availability of grants and other charitable funding.

FOR MORE INFORMATION

For information on careers, education and training, and internships, contact

American Association of Museums
1575 Eye Street, NW, Suite 400
Washington, DC 20005-1113
Tel: 202-289-1818
http://www.aam-us.org

This organization represents directors of the major art museums in North America. It sells a publication on professional practices, a salary survey, and a sample employment contract.

Association of Art Museum Directors
120 East 56th Street, Suite 520
New York, NY 10022-3673
Tel: 212-754-8084
http://www.aamd.org

Photographers

OVERVIEW

Photographers take and sometimes develop and print pictures of people, places, objects, and events, using a variety of cameras and photographic equipment. They work in the publishing, advertising, public relations, science, and business industries, as well as provide personal photographic services. They may also work as fine artists. There are approximately 129,000 photographers employed in the United States.

HISTORY

The word photograph means, "to write with light." Although the art of photography goes back only about 150 years, the two Greek words that were chosen and combined to refer to this skill quite accurately describe what it does.

The discoveries that led eventually to photography began early in the 18th century when a German scientist, Dr. Johann H. Schultze, experimented with the action of light on certain chemicals. He found that when these chemicals were covered by dark paper they did not change color but when they were exposed to sunlight, they darkened. A French painter named Louis Daguerre became the first photographer in 1839, using silver-iodide-coated plates and a small box. To develop images on the plates, Daguerre exposed them to mercury vapor. The daguerreotype, as these early photographs came to be known, took minutes to expose and the developing process was directly to the plate. There were no prints made.

Although the daguerreotype was the sensation of its day, it was not until George Eastman invented a simple camera and flexible roll film that photography began to come into widespread use in the late

1800s. After exposing this film to light and developing it with chemicals, the film revealed a color-reversed image, which is called a negative. To make the negative positive (aka: print a picture), light must be shone through the negative onto light-sensitive paper. This process can be repeated to make multiple copies of an image from one negative.

One of the most important developments in recent years is digital photography. In digital photography, instead of using film, pictures are recorded on microchips, which can then be downloaded onto a computer's hard drive. They can be manipulated in size, color, and shape, virtually eliminating the need for a darkroom. In the professional world, digital images are primarily used in electronic publishing and advertising since printing technology hasn't quite caught up with camera technology. However, printing technology is also advancing and even amateur photographers can use digital cameras and home printers to shoot, manipulate, correct, and print snapshots.

THE JOB

Photography is both an artistic and technical occupation. There are many variables in the process that a knowledgeable photographer can manipulate to produce a clear image or a more abstract work of fine art. First, photographers know how to use cameras and can adjust focus, shutter speeds, aperture, lenses, and filters. They know about the types and speeds of films. Photographers also know about light and shadow, deciding when to use available natural light and when to set up artificial lighting to achieve desired effects.

Some photographers send their film to laboratories, but some develop their own negatives and make their own prints. These processes require knowledge about chemicals such as developers and fixers and how to use enlarging equipment. Photographers must also be familiar with the large variety of papers available for printing photographs, all of which deliver a different effect. Most photographers continually experiment with photographic processes to improve their technical proficiency or to create special effects.

Digital photography is a rapidly growing technology. With digital photography, film is replaced by microchips that record pictures in digital format. Pictures can then be downloaded onto a computer's hard drive. Photographers use special software to manipulate the images on screen.

Photographers usually specialize in one of several areas: portraiture, commercial and advertising photography, photojournalism, fine art, educational photography, or scientific photography. There are subspecialties within each of these categories.

Art photographers, for example, use photography as a vehicle for artistic expression. The work of art photographers is collected by those with a special interest in the field, shown in galleries, and displayed in museums of art. The work of well-known photographers in this field is often collected and published in book form. There is some overlap between this and other forms of photography. The work of some photographers who did not set out to create works of art is nevertheless considered to have great artistic value. This category can include portraiture and photojournalism, as well as landscape, nature, architecture, and still life photography.

Other subspecialties include *scientific photographers*, who specialize in aerial or underwater photography, and *commercial photographers*, who specialize in food or fashion photography.

Some photographers write for trade and technical journals, teach photography in schools and colleges, act as representatives of photographic equipment manufacturers, sell photographic equipment and supplies, produce documentary films, or do freelance work.

REQUIREMENTS

High School
While in high school, take as many art classes and photography classes that are available. Chemistry is useful for understanding developing and printing processes. You can learn about photo manipulation software and digital photography in computer classes, and business classes will help if you are considering a freelance career.

Postsecondary Training
A college education is not required to become a photographer, although college training probably offers the most promising assurance of success in fields such as industrial, news, or scientific photography. There are degree programs at the associate's, bachelor's, and master's levels.

To become a photographer, you should have a broad technical understanding of photography plus as much practical experience with cameras as possible. Take many different kinds of photographs with a variety of cameras and subjects. Learn how to develop photographs and, if possible, build your own darkroom or rent one. Experience in picture composition, cropping prints (cutting images to a desired size), enlarging, and retouching are all valuable.

A nature photographer in the Paria Canyon-Vermillion Cliffs Wilderness in Utah prepares to take a shot. *(Layne Kennedy, Corbis)*

Other Requirements

You should possess manual dexterity, good eyesight and color vision, and artistic ability to succeed in this line of work. You need an eye for form and line, an appreciation of light and shadow, and the ability to use imaginative and creative approaches to photographs or film, especially in commercial work. In addition, you should be patient and accurate and enjoy working with detail.

Self-employed (or freelance) photographers need good business skills. They must be able to manage their own studios, including hiring and managing assistants and other employees, keeping records, and maintaining photographic and business files. Marketing and sales skills are also important to a successful freelance photography business.

EXPLORING

Photography is a field that anyone with a camera can explore. To learn more about this career, you can join high school camera clubs, yearbook or newspaper staffs, photography contests, and community hobby groups. You can also seek a part-time or summer job in a camera shop or work as a developer in a laboratory or processing center.

EMPLOYERS

About 129,000 photographers work in the United States, more than half of those are self-employed. Most jobs for photographers are provided by photographic or commercial art studios; other employers include newspapers and magazines, radio and TV broadcasting, government agencies, and manufacturing firms. Colleges, universities, and other educational institutions employ photographers to prepare promotional and educational materials.

STARTING OUT

Some photographers enter the field as apprentices, trainees, or assistants. Trainees may work in a darkroom, camera shop, or developing laboratory. They may move lights and arrange backgrounds for a commercial or portrait photographer or motion picture photographer. Assistants spend many months learning this kind of work before they move into a job behind a camera.

Many large cities have schools of photography, which may be a good way to start in the field. Beginning press photographers may work for one of the many newspapers and magazines published in their area. Other photographers choose to go into business for themselves as soon as they have finished their formal education. Setting up a studio may not require a large capital outlay, but beginners may find that success does not come easily.

ADVANCEMENT

Because photography is such a diversified field, there is no usual way in which to get ahead. Those who begin by working for someone else may advance to owning their own businesses. Commercial photographers may gain prestige as more of their pictures are placed in well-known trade journals or popular magazines. Press photographers may advance in salary and the kinds of important news stories assigned to them. A few photographers may become celebrities in their own right by making contributions to the art world or the sciences.

EARNINGS

The U.S. Department of Labor reports that salaried photographers earned median annual salaries of $26,170 in 2006. Salaries ranged from less than $15,540 to more than $56,640. Photographers who were employed by newspaper, book, and directory publishers earned mean annual salaries of $37,800 in 2006, while those employed by colleges and universities earned $40,990.

Self-employed photographers often earn more than salaried photographers, but their earnings depend on general business conditions. In addition, self-employed photographers do not receive the benefits that a company provides its employees.

Photographers in salaried jobs usually receive benefits such as paid holidays, vacations, and sick leave, and medical insurance.

WORK ENVIRONMENT

Work conditions vary based on the job and employer. Many photographers work a 35- to 40-hour workweek, but freelancers and news photographers often put in long, irregular hours. Commercial and portrait photographers work in comfortable surroundings. Photojournalists seldom are assured physical comfort in their work and may in fact face danger when covering stories on natural disasters or military conflicts. Some photographers work in research laboratory settings; others work on aircraft; and still others work underwater. For some photographers, conditions change from day to day. One day, they may be photographing a hot and dusty rodeo; the next they may be taking pictures of a dog sled race in Alaska.

In general, photographers work under pressure to meet deadlines and satisfy customers. Freelance photographers have the added pressure of uncertain incomes and have to continually seek out new clients.

For specialists in fields such as fashion photography, breaking into the field may take years. Working as another photographer's assistant is physically demanding when carrying equipment is required.

For freelance photographers, the cost of equipment can be quite expensive, with no assurance that the money spent will be repaid through income from future assignments. Freelancers in travel-related photography, such as travel and tourism photographers and photojournalists, have the added cost of transportation and accommodations. For all photographers, flexibility is a major asset.

OUTLOOK

Employment of photographers will increase about as fast as the average for all occupations through 2014, according to the *Occupational*

Outlook Handbook. The demand for new images should remain strong in education, communication, entertainment, marketing, and research. As the Internet grows and more newspapers and magazines turn to electronic publishing, demand will increase for photographers to produce digital images. Additionally, as the population grows and many families have more disposable income to spend, the demand should increase for photographers who specialize in portraiture, especially of children.

Photography is a highly competitive field. There are far more photographers than positions available. Only those who are extremely talented and highly skilled can support themselves as self-employed photographers. Many photographers take pictures as a sideline while working another job.

FOR MORE INFORMATION

The ASMP promotes the rights of photographers, educates its members in business practices, and promotes high standards of ethics.
American Society of Media Photographers (ASMP)
150 North Second Street
Philadelphia, PA 19106-1912
Tel: 215-451-2767
http://www.asmp.org

The NPPA maintains a job bank, provides educational information, and makes insurance available to its members. It also publishes News Photographer *magazine.*
National Press Photographers Association (NPPA)
3200 Croasdaile Drive, Suite 306
Durham, NC 27705-2588
Tel: 919-383-7246
Email: info@nppa.org
http://www.nppa.org

For information on nature photography, contact
North American Nature Photography Association
10200 West 44th Avenue, Suite 304
Wheat Ridge, CO 80033-2840
Tel: 303-422-8527
http://www.nanpa.org

This organization provides training, publishes its own magazine, and offers various services for its members.

Professional Photographers of America
229 Peachtree Street, NE, Suite 2200
Atlanta, GA 30303-1608
Tel: 800-786-6277
Email: csc@ppa.com
http://www.ppa.com

Visual Artists

QUICK FACTS

School Subjects
Art
History

Personal Skills
Artistic
Communication/ideas

Work Environment
Indoors and outdoors
One location with some
  travel

Minimum Education Level
High school diploma

Salary Range
$14,130 to $41,970 to
  $79,390+

Certification or Licensing
None available

Outlook
About as fast as the average

DOT
144, 779

GOE
01.04.01, 01.06.01

NOC
5136, 5244

O*NET-SOC
27-1012.00, 27-1013.01,
  27-1013.04, 27-1014.00,
  51-9195.05

OVERVIEW

Visual artists convey thoughts, opinions, and ideas through their work, whether it is a realistic painting, a piece of pottery, or an abstract sculpture. They use one or more media, such as clay, paint, metal, or computer technology, to create two- or three-dimensional works. The field of visual arts is usually separated into three categories: commercial art, fine art, and craft. There are approximately 208,000 visual artists employed in the United States, and about 63 percent of them are self-employed.

HISTORY

The history of art is a huge topic that covers thousands of years of human history all over the world. Many people devote their entire careers to its study, and since art history is such a large topic, historians usually specialize, focusing on either a time period, such as the Renaissance or the early 20th century, or a particular area, such as Mexico or Southeast Asia.

Anthropologists and historians speculate that the earliest works of art were created for their function rather than for decorative or aesthetic value. The Venus of Willendorf, a figure carved from limestone around 21,000 to 25,000 B.C., might have been a part of fertility rites and rituals. The cave paintings of France and Spain, which date back to 15,000 B.C., were probably ceremonial, meant to bring good luck to the hunt.

Much of early visual art was religious, reflecting the beliefs and legends with which people tried to understand their place in the world and in life. Art was also political, used to glorify society or the

182

leaders of society. For example, the immense sculptures of Ramses II of ancient Egypt and the sculptures of Roman art depicted their rulers and their stature in society.

The art of Greece and Rome exerted a profound influence on much of the history of Western art. The sculptural ideals developed by the ancient Greeks, particularly with their perfection of anatomical forms, continued to dominate Western sculpture until well into the 19th century. In painting, artists sought methods to depict or suggest a greater realism, experimenting with techniques of lighting, shading, and perspective.

The rise of the Christian era brought a return to symbolism over realism. Illuminated manuscripts, which were written texts, usually religious in content, and decorated with designs and motifs meant to provide further understanding of the text, became the primary form of artistic expression for nearly a millennium. The artwork for these manuscripts often featured highly elaborate and detailed abstract designs. The human figure was absent in much of this work, reflecting religious prohibition of the creation of idols.

Artists returned to more naturalistic techniques during the 14th century with the rise of Gothic art forms. The human figure returned to art and artists began creating works not only for rulers and religious institutions, but also for a growing wealthy class. Portrait painting became an increasingly important source of work and income for artists. New materials, particularly oil glazes and paints, allowed artists to achieve more exact detailing and more subtle light, color, and shading effects.

During the Renaissance, artists rediscovered the art of ancient Greece and Rome. This brought new developments not only in artists' techniques but also in their stature in society. The development of perspective techniques in the 14th and 15th centuries revolutionized painting. Perspective allowed the artists to create the illusion of three dimensions, so that a spectator felt that he or she looked not merely at a painting but into it. Advances in the study of anatomy enabled artists to create more dramatic and realistic figures, whether in painting or sculpture, providing the illusion of action and fluidity and heightening the naturalism of their work. Artists achieved higher status and were sought out by the wealthy, the church, and rulers for their talent and skill.

Renaissance artists became bolder and experimented with line, color, contour, shading, setting, and composition, presenting work of greater realism and at the same time of deeper emotional content. The style of an artist became more highly individualized, more a personal reflection of the artist's thoughts, beliefs, ideas, and feelings.

Artists continued to influence one another, but national and cultural differences began to appear in art as the Catholic Church lost its dominance and new religious movements took hold during the 16th and 17th centuries. Art academies, such as the Royal Academy of Painting and Sculpture in Paris, were established and sought to codify artistic ideals.

During the next two centuries there were profound changes in the nature of art, leading to the revolutionary work of the impressionists of the late 19th century and the dawn of the modern era in art. Sculpture, which had remained largely confined to the Greek and Roman ideals, found new directions. The individual sensibility of the artist took on a greater importance and led to a greater freedom of painting techniques. Many of the ideals of the French academy were challenged, leading to the avant-garde work of the early French impressionists. Artists began to take on a new role by presenting society with new concepts, ideas, and visions and radical departures in style. Artists no longer simply reflected prevailing culture but adopted leadership positions in creating culture, often rejecting entirely the artistic principles of the past.

The image of the artist as cultural outsider, societal misfit, or even tormented soul took hold. Artists working in the avant-garde achieved notoriety, if not financial reward, and the "misunderstood" or "starving" artist became a popular 20th-century image.

The 20th century witnessed an explosion of artistic styles and techniques. Art, both in painting and sculpture, became increasingly abstracted from reality, and purely formal concerns developed. Impressionism and postimpressionism gave way to futurism, expressionism, fauvism, cubism, nonobjective art, surrealism, and other styles.

American art, which had largely followed the examples set by European artists, came into its own during the 1940s and 1950s, with the rise of abstract expressionism. During the 1950s, a new art form, pop art, reintroduced recognizable images and often mundane objects to satirize and otherwise comment on cultural and societal life.

More recent trends in art have given the world the graffiti-inspired works of Keith Haring and the "non-art" sculpture of Jeff Koons, as well as the massive installations of Christo. Artists today work in a great variety of styles, forms, and media. Many artists combine elements of painting, sculpture, and other art forms, such as photography, music, and dance, into their work. The rise of video recording techniques and especially of three-dimensional computer animations has recently begun to challenge many traditional ideas of art.

This brief art history time line has covered only Western fine art, but different art trends and developments occurred around the world simultaneously. Europeans had acquired art objects from other parts of the world for centuries as curios, status symbols, and collectors' items, but the appreciation of these objects and paintings as works of art is relatively recent. Westerners now recognize paintings, sculpture, and functional objects from even the remotest parts of the world as having great artistic value and making significant contributions to the development of Western art.

The debate continues about whether some functional items, such as pottery, furniture, rugs, and jewelry, for example, can be considered works of art. The lines have become blurred between artistry and craftsmanship, since many objects created for a specific function are beautiful to look at, make social and cultural commentary, or push the limits of convention as much as any painting or sculpture. Many media forms traditionally considered craft media, such as woodworking, ceramics, silversmithing, and papier mâché, are used in sculpture and mixed-media works, further confusing the distinctions between art and craft.

Early commercial art may have its beginnings with signage, when symbols and pictures were used along with lettering to advertise places of business. Commercial art began to flourish with the advent of printing technology and the subsequent development of the publishing industry. Artists illustrated stories and advertisements and arranged type and artwork for books, magazines, and newspapers. The growth of the advertising industry throughout the 19th and 20th centuries fueled the growth of commercial art. Artists used black and white line art in the beginning, which gave way to color drawings, and then photography, and then computer-generated visuals. Today commercial artists work in all phases of publishing, including decorative and explanatory illustration, photography, layout, typography, and print production. Advertising art includes art direction, print advertising (magazines, newspapers, catalogs, and direct mail), package design, film production, and Web design.

THE JOB

Visual artists use their creative abilities to produce original works of art to express ideas; to provide social and cultural commentary; to communicate messages; to record events; to explore color, texture, line, and other visual elements; and for many other purposes. *Fine artists* usually create works for display in public areas or in private galleries. *Commercial artists* produce art that illustrates, explains, or draws attention to text, as in advertising and publishing. *Craft workers,* or *artisans,* create works that usually have a function.

Fine artists work for themselves. Their art comes from their own ideas and methods of working. They spend years developing their own style, focusing on a chosen subject, and refining their skills in a particular medium. Many artists work in only one technique or focus on one subject area throughout their lives, such as painting only large-scale oil portraits. Most artists change styles subtly as they gain experience in their art and in their lives, and some experiment with different media. For example, a sculptor who works in clay may switch to bronze casting later in his or her career. Many artists develop a particular style and apply that style across a broad range of techniques, from painting to etching to sculpture.

Painters use different media to paint a variety of subjects, such as landscapes, people, or objects. They work with oil paint, acrylic paint, tempera, watercolors, gouache, pen and ink, or pastels, but they may also incorporate such nontraditional media as clay, paper, cloth, and a variety of other material. They use brushes, palette knives, airbrushes, and other tools to apply color to canvas, paper, or other surfaces. Painters use line, texture, color, and other visual elements to produce the desired effect.

Sculptors create three-dimensional works of art. They may carve objects from stone, plaster, concrete, or wood. They may use their fingers to model clay or wax into objects. Some sculptors create forms from metal or stone, using various masonry tools and equipment. Some sculptors form objects with clay or wax from which to make a mold, which is then cast in bronze or other metals, plastics, or other materials. Others create works from found objects, whether parts of a car, branches of a tree, or other items. Like painters, sculptors may be identified with a particular technique or style. Their work can take monumental forms, or they may work on a very small scale.

Visual artists also include *printmakers,* who engrave, etch, or mask their designs on wood, stone, metal, or silk screen. These designs are then transferred, or printed, on paper. Printmakers can also create their art using computers. These artists use computer scanners to scan the prepared plates and then reproduce prints using high-quality color printers.

Mixed-media artists incorporate several techniques, such as painting, sculpture, collage, printing, and drawing, into one work of art.

Ceramic artists, also known as *potters, ceramists, sculptors,* and *clay artists,* work with clay to make both functional objects and sculpture. Their work often blurs the distinction between fine art and craft. They blend basic elements (such as clay and water) and more specialized components (such as texture fillers, colorants, and talc) and form the mixture into shapes using either manual techniques or wheel-throwing techniques to create dinnerware, vases, beads, tiles, architectural installations, and sculptures. Some ceramic artists make molds from materials like plaster and use a casting method. The formed pieces, called greenware, are fired in kilns at very high temperatures. The artists apply glazes and other finishes and fire them again to set the pieces.

Other visual artists that blur the distinction between fine art and craft are *glass workers,* including *stained glass artists, glassblowers, and etchers.* Stained glass artists cut colored pieces of glass, arrange them in a design, and connect them with leading. The leading is then soldered to hold the glass pieces together. Glassblowers use a variety of instruments to blow molten glass into bottles, vases, and sculptures. Etchers use fine hand and power tools, and sometimes chemicals, to create a design in the surface of glass.

Fiber artists create wall hangings and sculpture from textiles, threads, and paper.

Visual artists are innovators and are not bound by tradition or convention. They respond to cultural and societal stimuli and incorporate them into works of art. In recent years, they have used copiers, laser beams, computers, and other technology not originally intended for art as alternative media.

Multimedia artists create art for commercial and fine art purposes by combining traditional artistic skills with new technologies such as computers, scanners, and digital cameras.

Most fine artists work on their own. Once they create a body of work, they usually seek out a gallery to display and sell their work. The gallery owner and artist set the prices for pieces of art, and the gallery owner receives a commission on any work that sells. The relationship between the gallery owner and artist is often one of close cooperation. For example, a gallery owner may encourage artists to explore new techniques, styles, and ideas while helping to establish their reputation. As an artist becomes well-known, selling his or her work often becomes easier, and many well-known artists receive commissions for their art. A sculptor, for example, might be commissioned to create a piece specifically for the lobby or outdoor plaza of a public building. A stained glass artist might be commissioned to make a window for a church.

Commercial artists include *graphic designers, illustrators, art directors, and photographers.* Their art differs from fine art in that it is usually created according to the wishes of a client or employer. Computers are now widely used to create illustrations, typography, and page

An artist creates a sculpture. *(Peter Beck, Corbis)*

layouts, but traditional methods are still being used for illustration. Original drawings, paintings, collage, and other two-dimensional pieces can be scanned and digitized and then the image can be manipulated using software programs. Commercial artists work primarily in the advertising and publishing industries and for businesses that need advertising and publishing services, such as retail stores.

In most cases, commercial art is closely related to textual matter. For example, a medical illustrator might draw a series of pictures to demonstrate a surgical technique. Advertisements often show a product, or someone using a product, along with text that persuades viewers to buy that product. Photographs accompany feature articles in magazines and newspapers to show the people and places depicted in the story. Art is also included to draw the reader's attention to certain textual matter. Art directors and graphic designers commission, select, and arrange visuals and text on the page so it will be easy to read as well as attractive and pleasing to the reader.

Craft workers are artists who make decorative, usually three-dimensional items that are often functional. They make jewelry, furniture, dinnerware, musical instruments, pottery, and quilts, to name a few. They use many of the same techniques as fine artists, including painting, carving, casting, and modeling, and they use a variety of tools from needle and thread to chain saws.

Another specialized area of visual art is evaluation and restoration. Painting experts preserve and restore aged, faded, or damaged art. They also evaluate the age and authenticity of the work. Restoring art can be tedious and detailed work, requiring the precise and skillful application of solvents and cleaning agents to the work. *Art conservators* also repair damaged sculpture, pottery, jewelry, fabrics, and other items, depending on their area of expertise.

Visual art is an intensely personal endeavor. Most artists are people with a desire and need to explore visual representations of real and imagined worlds. Their work usually continues and develops throughout their lives. Creating art is rarely a career choice but rather a way of life.

REQUIREMENTS

High School

In the public school system, there is very little art instruction at the elementary level, so high school is your chance to take as many art courses as you can. Many schools offer general art instruction that exposes you to several techniques and principles. Some schools offer specialized art classes in painting, sculpture, design principles, graphic design, photography, and computer graphics. You may have to find other art instruction outside of your school if you are interested in ceramics, woodworking, stained glass, or another specialty. Check community centers, junior colleges, independent schools of art, or local galleries that might offer classes.

Postsecondary Training

There are no formal educational requirements for becoming a visual artist. However, most artists benefit from training, and many, about

90 percent, attend art schools or programs in colleges and universities. Of all artists, about 20 percent major in fine arts, according to the American Institute of Graphic Arts, and of those, 20 percent have at least a master's degree. Master's programs may offer majors in ceramic art, fiber art, art history, film and photography, sculpture, and a number of others.

Two-year or associate's degree programs are available in many art specialties, including computer graphics, advertising design, fashion design, illustration, and photography, among others.

Besides earning a degree, there are many workshops, private studios, and individuals that offer instruction, practice, and exposure to art and the works and ideas of other artists. It is wise to learn a variety of techniques, be exposed to as many media and styles as possible, and gain an understanding of the history and theory of art. By learning as much as possible, you will have more choices for your own artistic expression.

Some types of artists need training in an additional field. For example, medical illustrators are required to have training in biology and anatomy. Medical or scientific illustrators not only have a four-year degree in art with an emphasis in premedical courses, but most have a master's degree in medical illustration. Only a few schools in the United States offer this specialized coursework.

Apprenticeships are sometimes available in certain art fields, such as glassmaking, ceramics, printmaking, woodworking, and papermaking. Apprenticeships allow young artists the opportunity for intensive training under master artists while actually producing art objects.

Other Requirements

While attending classes, earning a degree, or working under a master artist, it is important for fine artists and craft workers to build a body of work that shows a definite and unique style and a thematic progression. Gallery owners and sales representatives want to represent artists they can count on to keep producing work. They also like to see a certain amount of consistency of style to satisfy customer demand for a particular artist's work. Commercial artists need to build a portfolio of published work to show to potential clients and employers. A portfolio can be very specific—showing only portrait photography, for example—or it can be general, showing your ability to use a number of techniques for varied clients.

You need creativity and imagination to be a visual artist, but you also need patience, persistence, determination, independence, sensitivity, and confidence in your abilities.

Because earning a living as a fine artist or craft worker is very difficult, especially when you are starting out, you may have to work at another job. With the proper training and educational background, many fine artists are able to work in art-related positions, such as art teachers, art directors, or graphic designers, while pursuing their art activities independently.

EXPLORING

You need very little to begin to explore your interest in art. Crayons, pencil and paper, glue and found objects can get you started. Inexpensive paints, clays, markers, and other supplies are available at art supply stores and department stores.

Your school may have art-related clubs, such as poster clubs and drama clubs, that allow you to design and construct sets and costumes, and publicity committees. School newspapers and magazines will give you exposure to commercial art, including illustration, photography, and page design.

Specialized art instruction may be available at community centers, art galleries, and private studios in your town.

Visit art galleries and museums often and begin to form opinions about what you like and don't like, both in terms of design and technique. Visit your library and look at art books and magazines that feature the art of particular periods or artists. There are also numerous resources that give step-by step instructions for art techniques.

The New York Foundation for the Arts hosts a valuable Web site (http://www.nyfa.org) that offers information on job leads, art events, and other concerns of visual artists.

EMPLOYERS

Fine artists are usually self-employed, and very few are able to support themselves completely by the sale of their art. They hold other jobs that allow them to pursue their artistic endeavors on a part-time basis, or they may work in art-related jobs, such as in teaching, commercial art, art therapy, or working in a gallery or art museum.

Most craft workers are also self-employed, although there are full-time positions in some fields. For example, a stained-glass artist might find a job with a small shop, or a ceramic artist might work for a pottery production factory.

Many commercial artists are self-employed, but they can more readily find full-time employment, primarily in the publishing and

Books to Read: Career and Educational Resources

Camenson, Blythe. *Great Jobs for Art Majors*. 2d ed. New York: McGraw-Hill, 2003.

Cox, Mary. *2007 Artist's & Graphic Designer's Market*. Cincinnati, Ohio: Writers Digest Books, 2006.

Gulrich, Kathy. *187 Tips for Artists: How to Create a Successful Art Career—and Have Fun in the Process!* New York: Center City Publishing, 2003.

Hoving, Thomas. *Art for Dummies*. Hoboken, N.J.: John Wiley & Sons, 1999.

Lerner, Ralph E., and Judith Bresler. *Art Law: The Guide for Collectors, Investors, Dealers, and Artists*. 3d ed. New York: Practising Law Institute, 2005.

Michels, Caroll. *How to Survive and Prosper as an Artist: Selling Yourself Without Selling Your Soul*. 5th ed. New York: Owl Books, 2001.

Moore, Sean. *How to Make Money as an Artist: The 7 Winning Strategies of Successful Fine Artists*. Chicago: Chicago Review Press, 2000.

National Association of Schools of Art and Design. *National Association of Schools of Art and Design Directory 2007*. Reston, Va.: National Association of Schools of Art and Design, 2007.

Preble, Duane, Sarah Preble, and Patrick L. Frank. *Artforms: An Introduction to the Visual Arts*. 7th ed. Upper Saddle River, N.J.: Prentice Hall, 2001.

Smith, Constance. *Art Marketing 101: A Handbook for the Fine Artist*. 3d ed. Nevada City, Calif.: ArtNetwork, 2007.

advertising industries. They also work in all kinds of businesses, including retail, public relations, fashion, and entertainment.

STARTING OUT

Visual artists interested in exhibiting or selling their products should first and foremost develop a portfolio, or a collection of work. The portfolio, which should be carefully organized to showcase a wide variety of the artist's talent and capabilities, is an essential tool when looking for work.

To develop business opportunities, artists should investigate their potential markets. Reference books, such as the *2007 Artist's &*

Graphic Designer's Market (Cincinnati, Ohio: Writers Digest Books, 2006) may be helpful, as well as library books that offer information on business and tax law and related issues.

Local fairs and art shows often provide opportunities for new artists to display their work. Art councils are a good source of information on upcoming fairs. However, most successful artists are represented by a gallery or agent that displays their work and approaches potential buyers when new works are available. The gallery or agent gets a commission for each piece of artwork sold. Relationships between artists and gallery operators can be tricky, so legal advice is recommended, but such relationships can also be beneficial to both creator and seller. A good gallery operator encourages, supports, and believes in the artists he or she represents.

Many art schools and universities have placement services to help graduates find jobs. Although fine artists are generally self-employed, many need to work at another job, at least initially, to support themselves while they establish a reputation.

ADVANCEMENT

The channels of advancement for self-employed fine artists are not as well-defined as they would be for an artist employed at a company. An artist may become increasingly well-known, both nationally and internationally, and may be able to command higher prices for his or her work. The success of a fine artist depends on a variety of factors, including talent, drive, and determination. However, luck often seems to play a role in many artists' successes, and some artists do not achieve recognition until late in life, if at all. Artists with business skills may open galleries to display their own and others' work. Those with the appropriate educational backgrounds may become art teachers, agents, or critics.

Commercial artists can start out in publishing or advertising as graphic designers and with experience become art directors or account executives.

EARNINGS

The amount of money earned by visual artists varies greatly. Because most work as freelancers, they can set their own prices.

According to the U.S. Department of Labor, the median annual earnings of salaried fine artists, including painters and sculptors, were $41,970 in 2006. Salaries ranged from less than $18,350 to more than $79,390. Salaries for craft artists ranged from less than $14,130 to $46,700 or more annually. Multimedia artists had median annual earnings of $51,350.

Artists often work long hours and earn little, especially when they are first starting out. The price they charge is up to them, but much depends on the value the public places on their work. A particular item may sell for a few dollars or tens of thousands of dollars, or at any price in between. Often the value of a piece may increase considerably after it has been sold. Artwork that may have earned an artist only a few hundred dollars when it was first completed may earn many thousands of dollars the next time it is sold if the artist's work becomes well-known and in demand.

Some artists obtain grants that allow them to pursue their art; others win prizes and awards in competitions. Most artists, however, have to work on their projects part time while holding a regular, full-time job. Many artists teach in art schools, high schools, or out of their studios. Artists who sell their products must pay Social Security and other taxes on any money they receive and provide their own benefits.

WORK ENVIRONMENT

Most painters and sculptors work out of their homes or in studios. Some work in small areas in their apartments or homes; others work in large, well-ventilated lofts, garages, or warehouse space. An artist may choose complete solitude to work; others thrive on interaction with other artists and people. Occasionally, painters and sculptors work outside. Artists engaged in monumental work, particularly sculptors, often have helpers who assist in the creation of a piece of art, working under the artist's direction. They may contract with a foundry to cast a finished sculpture in bronze, iron, or another metal. In addition, artists often work at fairs, shops, museums, and other places where their work is being exhibited.

Artists often work long hours, and those who are self-employed do not have the security of a steady paycheck, paid vacations, insurance coverage, or any of the other benefits usually offered by a company or firm. However, artists are able to work at their own pace, set their own prices, and make their own decisions. The energy and creativity that go into an artist's work bring feelings of pride and satisfaction. Most artists genuinely love what they do.

OUTLOOK

Employment for visual artists is expected to grow as fast as the average for all occupations through 2014, according to the U.S. Department of Labor. However, because they are usually self-employed, much of their success depends on the amount and type of work created, the drive and determination in selling the artwork, and the interest or readiness of the public to appreciate and purchase the work. Continued population growth, higher incomes, and increased appreciation for fine art will create a demand for visual artists.

Success for an artist, however, is difficult to quantify. Individual artists may consider themselves successful as their talent matures and they are better able to present their vision in their work. This type of success goes beyond financial considerations. Few artists enter this field for the money. Financial success depends on many factors, many of which have nothing to do with the artist or his or her work. Artists with good marketing skills or the ability to hire someone with marketing expertise will likely be the most successful in selling their work. Although artists should not let their style be dictated by market trends, those interested in financial success can attempt to determine what types of artwork the public wants.

It often takes several years for an artist's work and reputation to be established. Many artists have to support themselves through other employment. There are numerous employment opportunities for commercial artists in such fields as publishing, advertising, fashion and design, entertainment, and teaching, although there is strong competition from others who are attracted to these fields. Freelancers may have difficulty selling their work until they establish their artistic reputation. Artists skilled in computer techniques will have an edge.

This occupation may be affected by the amount of funding granted by the government. The National Endowment for the Arts, for example, awards grants and funding to help talented artists hone their craft.

FOR MORE INFORMATION

This national, nonprofit educational organization promotes and understanding of American craft. Its Web site offers an overview of craft art, membership opportunities, useful publications, and a list of craft shows and markets.

American Craft Council
72 Spring Street, 6th Floor
New York, NY 10012-4019
Tel: 212-274-0630
Email: council@craftcouncil.org
http://www.craftcouncil.org

The following organization helps artists market and sell their art. It offers marketing tools, a newsletter, a directory of artists, and reference resources.

ArtNetwork
PO Box 1360
Nevada City, CA 95959-1360
Tel: 530-470-0862
Email: info@artmarketing.com
http://www.artmarketing.com

Visit the center's Web site for a database of undergraduate and graduate sculpture programs, profiles of famous sculptors, a message board, and an online directory of selected works and credentials of ISC member sculptors. Student sculptors can post a mini portfolio at the site for free.

International Sculpture Center (ISC)
19 Fairgrounds Road, Suite B
Hamilton, NJ 08619-3447
Tel: 609-689-1051
http://www.sculpture.org

For general information on arts study, contact

National Art Education Association
1916 Association Drive
Reston, VA 20191-1590
Tel: 703-860-8000
Email: info@naea-reston.org
http://www.naea-reston.org

Visit the NASAD's Web site for information on educational programs.

National Association of Schools of Art and Design (NASAD)
11250 Roger Bacon Drive, Suite 21
Reston, VA 20190-5248
Tel: 703-437-0700
Email: info@arts-accredit.org
http://nasad.arts-accredit.org

For education information, contact

National Council on Education for the Ceramic Arts
77 Erie Village Square, Suite 280
Erie, CO 80516-6996
Tel: 866-266-2322

Email: office@nceca.net
http://www.nceca.net

The NEA was established by Congress in 1965 to support excellence in the arts. It offers grants to artists and arts organizations, as well as various community-based programs. Visit its Web site for more information.
National Endowment for the Arts (NEA)
1100 Pennsylvania Avenue, NW
Washington, DC 20506-0001
Tel: 202-682-5400
Email: webmgr@arts.endow.gov
http://arts.endow.gov

The NSS is the oldest organization of professional sculptors in the United States. Contact it for information on membership, scholarships, and competitions.
National Sculpture Society (NSS)
237 Park Avenue
New York, NY 10017-0010
Tel: 212-764-5645
http://www.sculpturereview.com/nss.html

The following organization provides an information exchange and sharing of professional opportunities:
Sculptors Guild
110 Greene Street, Suite 601
New York, NY 10012-3838
Tel: 212-431-5669
Email: sculptorsguild@gmail.com
http://www.sculptorsguild.org

For information on scholarships for high school seniors and college students and mentoring programs for inner-city artists ages 14 to 20, contact
Worldstudio Foundation
200 Varick Street, Suite 507
New York, NY 10014-7041
Email: info@worldstudio.org
http://www.worldstudio.org

Index

Entries and page numbers in bold indicate major treatment of a topic.